C000046119

BIRDS

OF

CHINA

INCLUDING HONG KONG

JOHN MACKINNON
AND NIGEL HICKS

NEW HOLLAND

Reprinted in 2003

This edition published in 2001 by
New Holland Publishers (UK) Ltd
London • Cape Town • Sydney • Auckland

www.newhollandpublishers.com

Garfield House, 86 Edgware Road, London W2 2EA, United Kingdom
80 McKenzie Street, Cape Town 8001, South Africa
14 Aquatic Drive, Frenchs Forest, NSW 2086, Australia
218 Lake Road, Northcote, Auckland, New Zealand

First published in 1996

ISBN 1 85974 969 0

Editors: Jo Hemmings and David A. Christie
Assistant Editor: Sophie Bessemer
Design and Cartography by D & N Publishing, Hungerford, Berkshire
except map p.8 by Carte Blanche, Basingstoke, Hampshire
Illustration (p.5): David Daly
Index: J. E. Bailey

Reproduction by Modern Age Repro House Limited, Hong Kong
Printed and bound in Malaysia by Times Offset (M) Sdn Bhd

Front cover photograph: Asian Fairy-bluebird (Nigel Hicks)
Title page photograph: Omeishan Liocichla (Nigel Hicks)

Acknowledgements
All the photographs in this book were taken by Nigel Hicks and John
MacKinnon with the exception of the following:
David M. Cottridge (14l, 17u, 50u, 51l, 53u, 122lr, 126u, 127l, 133u, 134l);
Gerald Cubitt (44u); Tim Loseby (78u, 85u, 95l); D. S. Melville (56l, 70l); Peter
Morris (137l, 138l); Nature Photographers: Mark Bolton (36l), Hugh Miles
(58ul), Roger Tidman (35lr, 36ur, 128l); Michael Pitts (19u); Morten Strange
(65l); Ray Tipper (18l, 35ur, 50l, 52u, 54u); Windrush Photos: Göran Ekström
(131u), John Hollis (122u), David Tipling (14u, 31u, 31m, 35ll, 36ul, 37u, 59u,
80u, 85l, 95u), B. Van den Beo (56u); WWF Hong Kong: (52l, 55u, 57u).

    John MacKinnon would like to thank various people who have been of general
assistance in the preparation of this book – World Wide Fund for Nature (WWF) who
have sponsored most of the author's fieldwork in China; Ministry of Forestry, Beijing,
who manage the nature reserve system and have been partners in most of the field sur-
veys; WWF Hong Kong, and in particular the successive directors Mary Ketterer and
David Melville, who have provided a base, beds and office space for the author in Hong
Kong for serveral years; Dr Ken Searle for his enthusiasm for Chinese birds and allow-
ing free range of the Hong Kong park aviaries; Prof Wang Sung of the Institute of Zoology, Beijing, for his continued friendship and assistance and the many individuals in
specific reserves who have been of assistance over the last ten years.
    Nigel Hicks would like to thank a number of people who helped to make the
bird photography possible. In Hong Kong these people include Mr Stephen To of
Jardine Consumer Electronics for the loan of Canon camera equipment, Dr David
Melville and Llewellyn Young of the World Wide Fund for Nature for helping with
access to Mai Po Marshes Nature Reserve, Dr Ken Searle and Mr KK Lee for help
in the aviaries of the Hong Kong Botanical Garden, and Dr Gary Ades and Mr
Andrew McAulay of the Kadoorie Farm and Botanic Garden. In China, thanks go
to Prof Yang Yuanchang, Dr Zhou Xuesong and Mr Liu Jiazhu of the Southwest
Forestry College, Kunming, for their help and companionship and to the staff of
the Qiqihar branch of the China International Travel Service for their assistance in
gaining access to the Zhalong Nature Reserve, Helongjiang province.

Contents

Introduction

China is one of the largest countries in the world, with a total area of ten million square kilometres, or 7% of the land surface of the planet. It is a huge country of great extremes, from the world's highest peak of Everest at 8848m to one of the world's lowest land points, at –155m in the Turpan basin, and from the permafrost of the extreme north to the tropical seas of the extreme south. Habitats include forests, grasslands, deserts and wetlands.

This great diversity of habitats, together with China's large size, gives rise to a great richness of biological diversity. China is ranked third richest country in the world in terms of its species – a remarkable state for a largely temperate land mass. In terms of birds, this richness is shown in over 1,300 species recorded from the country, including some of the most spectacular and fascinating birds in the world.

China also, however, has a huge human population of over one billion, mostly in the eastern half of the country, and pressure on natural habitats is very severe. Many wild species are threatened with extinction, while others are rare or restricted to very small distributions. Conservation of the remaining habitats of these species is urgent, but difficult. The Chinese government is, however, well aware of the importance of the task and has set aside over 600 areas as nature reserves, with more planned.

There are still a lot of gaps to be filled in our knowledge of the distributions of Chinese birds, and we hope that this modest book may help in encouraging more people to join in the work of documentation that is needed. The challenge is great, but rewards are also there. China is a wonderful place in which to get off the beaten track with a purpose. There are many new finds to be made, and even the humdrum is strange and new to most visitors.

A book of this size cannot be a complete or exhaustive guide to the birds of China. It does, however, serve as a broad introduction to the families of birds in China and gives descriptions and photos of both the most familiar or common birds of China as well as some of the species and endemic birds that are not so common but which the visiting birdwatcher may want to track down. Wide-ranging groups such as seabirds, shorebirds and birds of prey are given only minimal coverage, whilst truly Chinese groups such as babblers, pheasants and waterbirds are covered rather more fully.

Many look-alike species are referred to in the text with their distinguishing characters, but are not formally illustrated or described. Since China is one of the less well-known parts of the ornithological world, and the book contains some species never previously illustrated photographically, the book should be of interest to both the novice and the experienced birdwatcher.

How to use this book

This guide has been designed for easy identification of the characteristic birds of China.

Photographs tend to be of adult males, but photos of females and young are included where these may need clearer illustration. Flight views are given of some species most often seen in flight.

Use of family silhouettes helps the user to locate the right section of the book to find a given species. Each species description is headed by the common English and scientific names and the total body length in centimetres. Many synonyms remain in common use, but the nomenclature is standardized more or less to follow Sibley and Monroe's 1989 classification; the family sequence, however, follows that used by Madge and Brazil *Identification Guide to the Birds of the Eastern Palearctic* (Christopher Helm, in prep.).

Descriptions give an overall account of the appearance of each species and include additional useful information on characteristic behaviour, calls and habitat use that will also help in identification. A brief note on the distribution and status of each species helps to eliminate other species and will also help birdwatchers to decide where to go to look for particular birds. The distribution maps should be used to check whether the species can be expected at the given locality. A habitat map of China is included to show the main vegetation types of the country and regionalization used in distribution descriptions.

Parts of a bird

The preceding illustration shows the main parts of a bird used in descriptions of plumage and anatomy. It is useful to familiarize yourself thoroughly with these terms rather than have to look up the parts of a bird each time you read a description.

It is also useful to be able to make your own field sketches of birds which you are not sure of, and to mark details of interesting or noted patterns or colour on different parts of the bird.

Glossary

basal At the base end of an appendage or feather
cere Bare fleshy base to bill on a hawk
coronal Along the top of the head or crown
distal Panel at the tip of a feather or appendage
endemic Confined to a particular small area
eyebrow Contrasting line above eye
eyestripe Contrasting line through eye
flank Side of the body
gape Unfeathered fleshy area at each corner of beak
gorget Band of contrasting colour across breast
gregarious Living in groups
lores Area between eye and bill
lower mandible Lower bill
malar area Side of face from bill below eye
mesial Down the centre of something, usually throat
nuchal crest Crest of feathers at base of nape
orbital Around the eye
pied Coloured black and white
rackets Extensions to a bird's tail with feathered endings
speculum Colour flash on a duck's wing
storey Canopy layer in a forest
subterminal Not quite at the end of a feather or appendage
terminal At the distal end of a feather or appendage
underwing Entire undersurface of wing
upper mandible Upper bill
vagrant Wandering out of its normal distribution
vent Area around anus including undertail-coverts
wing lining Feathers under base of wing

China's avifauna

China lists just over 1,300 species of bird recorded or expected in its huge territory. This includes a larger number than in any other temperate country in the world, plus a small inflation as a result of China's tropical southern fringe.

Most bird families have long and full lists of members, but there are some families and groups that are particularly Chinese. For instance, China is the centre of distribution of pheasants, with 62 species out of a global total of about 200.

Key to corner tabs

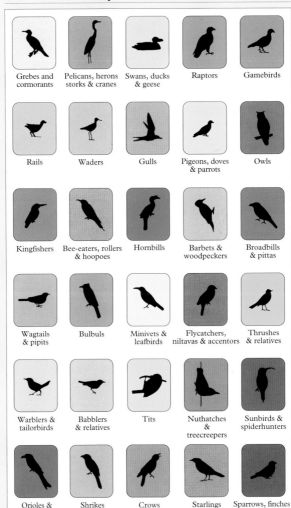

Grebes and cormorants	Pelicans, herons storks & cranes	Swans, ducks & geese	Raptors	Gamebirds
Rails	Waders	Gulls	Pigeons, doves & parrots	Owls
Kingfishers	Bee-eaters, rollers & hoopoes	Hornbills	Barbets & woodpeckers	Broadbills & pittas
Wagtails & pipits	Bulbuls	Minivets & leafbirds	Flycatchers, niltavas & accentors	Thrushes & relatives
Warblers & tailorbirds	Babblers & relatives	Tits	Nuthatches & treecreepers	Sunbirds & spiderhunters
Orioles & drongos	Shrikes	Crows	Starlings & mynas	Sparrows, finches & buntings

Another particularly Chinese group is the laughingthrushes, of which China boasts no fewer than 36 species, or more than half the world total. China is very rich in crows and rosefinches, and is also especially rich in ducks, swans and geese, its 50 species being about a quarter of the world total.

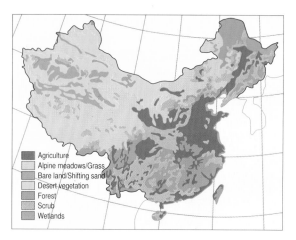

Agriculture
Alpine meadows/Grass
Bare land/Shifting sand
Desert vegetation
Forest
Scrub
Wetlands

Perhaps closest to the heart and culture of China, however, are the cranes. Nine of the world's 14 species live in China, breeding in the north and migrating in winter to the southern wetlands. The fantastic elegant dancing displays of the cranes, combined with their lifelong faithfulness and regularity of habits, have endeared them to the people and they have been revered in verse and art from the earliest times.

Not all attitudes towards birds are so noble and benign. Chinese cuisine is very varied, and eating wildlife is a strong feature. Pheasants, pigeons, thrushes and indeed almost every type of bird is good for the pot, and there are always many pots in China.

The present book describes and illustrates 252 species from a total of 54 families. The key on page 7 gives silhouettes to help the reader to locate the right family in the description section of the book.

Bird habitats of China

China has a huge range of habitats. These include the highest peaks in the world, the largest high-altitude plateau in the world, both hot and cold deserts, some of the world's most spectacular wetlands, great grassy steppes, seashores, and a range of forest types from permafrost tundra in the north-east, through temperate coniferous and broadleaf forests over most of eastern China, to tropical forests in the extreme south. Birds use all of these habitats, but each species uses only some of the wide range available. Recognizing habitat is a key to correct species identification.

Many birds in China show seasonal changes in distribution and/or habitat use, tending to live further north or higher up mountains in the summer months and migrating south or descending in altitude in winter. Indeed, the east coast of China is an important flyway for birds that breed in extreme northern latitudes but migrate south in winter. Some of these stay in the southern parts of China itself, whilst others fly on way south to equatorial regions of Indonesia.

The habitat map (left) shows the main habitat types used by birds and given in their descriptions in this book. The map is generalized and simplified. It should be appreciated that land relief is also significant. Where mountains stand out of an area which at sea level may support subtropical evergreen forests, the vegetation at higher altitudes will vary through montane formations, which often resemble vegetation of lower altitudes much further north. Thus, we find subalpine and alpine vegetation in tropical mountains, as well as in the extreme northern latitudes of the country.

The major vegetation types mapped are:

1. **Cultivated areas** are extensive in the east and south of the country. Such lands are mostly farmland but may contain woods, orchards and plantations, as well as land under fallow. All these provide habitat for some bird species, and in spring and autumn many migrants have to pass though these lands on passage.

2. **Alpine meadows** are extensive areas of the Tibetan plateau and smaller areas on some of the major mountain ranges of south-west and north-west China. They have a rather rich, though stunted, vegetation and a distinctive bird fauna including some rare mountain species. Grassy steppes form a wide swathe across northern China, being wetter and lusher in the east and becoming gradually drier to the west. Somewhat specialized grasslands grow on some of the loose loess soils in the Yellow River valley.

3. **Bare land** consists of areas of bare rock of generally great height or steepness, or areas of mobile sand dunes where there is no vegetation at all.

4. **Deserts** include three main types. Cold deserts are found on the Tibetan plateau at altitudes of over 4000m, where cold dry conditions limit the growth of plants; hot deserts fall into two types, sandy and stony. Each desert type has its own flora, and some plants spring into life on those rare occasions when it rains. The birds of desert are limited, but some species specialize in desert conditions.

5. **Forests**. These include several sorts:

Temperate coniferous forests, dominated by fir, spruce and hemlock at higher altitudes or by pines and larches at lower altitudes, but often mixed with birches and other broadleaf species.

Temperate broadleaf forests. These are mostly deciduous and dominated by oaks, beech, chestnuts and familiar European temperate genera.

Subtropical mixed forests. These are composed of hardleaved evergreen oaks and chestnuts mixed with some tropical pines and *Cunninghamia*.

Tropical evergreen and semi-evergreen forests. These rich formations are confined to the extreme south of the country and on south Taiwan and Hainan island. These forests are varied in composition and sometimes very tall and complex in structure.

6. **Scrub** includes a variety of secondary formations of low stature resulting from deforestation, fire or general degradation of vegetation caused by grazing and cutting. In the east of China, where most of the original forest has been cleared, these scrub areas provide the best cover for many bird species.

7. **Wetlands** include a wide range of types, from northern swampy marshes and lakes to the great lakes of the Yangtze valley, small alpine marshes of the Tibetan plateau, salt pans of Xinjiang in north-west China and mangroves and shorelines of the tropical south. In total area wetlands are not extensive and hardly show up on a vegetation map of this scale, but these are some of the most important areas for birds and many of the most spectacular and most endangered species in China are wetland specialists.

Administrative units of China

1 Xinjiang A. R.	12 Shaanxi	24 Inner Mongolia
2 Tibet	13 Shanxi	A. R.
(Xizang) A. R.	14 Henan	25 Jilin
3 Qinghai	15 Anhui	26 Heilongjiang
4 Gansu	16 Jiangxi	27 Ningxia
5 Sichuan	17 Fujian	28 Hainan Island
6 Yunnan	18 Zhejiang	29 Beijing
7 Guizhou	19 Shanghai	30 Tianjin
8 Guangxi A. R.	20 Jiangsu	31 Taiwan Island
9 Guangdong	21 Shandong	32 Hong Kong
10 Hunan	22 Hebei	
11 Hubei	23 Liaoning	

China is comprised of 32 administrative divisions. These include four autonomous regions, three municipalities, 24 provinces, plus the Special Administrative Unit of Hong Kong and the currently self-governing island of Taiwan. These are shown on the accompanying map, using the modern Pinyin system of anglicized names. In some cases, this book uses familiar English names such as Tibet for Xizang, Yangtze for Changjiang, Yellow River for Huanghe etc., because these names are more widely recognized by an English-language audience.

Some areas of territory claimed by China, including parts of south-eastern Tibet and large areas of China's seas, are under international dispute. The maps used in this book indicate the biological area covered and are not intended to have any political significance.

How to watch birds

The marvellous thing about birdwatching is that you can do it anywhere, at any time, and the pleasure is accumulative. The beginner needs only a small pair of binoculars and a notebook, whilst the dedicated twitcher will invest in all-weather clothes, expensive optical instruments and maybe sound-recording and playback equipment.

For general use, a pair of shower-proof 8×30 binoculars is adequate. Higher magnifications result in greater difficulty in locating birds quickly in the narrow field, greater weight, greater cost and more difficulty in holding the image steady. If you really need more magnification to view distant birds on lakes or coastlines, invest in a spotting-scope with a tripod.

In China, birds are extensively hunted and are generally rather shy. Look for quiet places and remain partially concealed. Sit still when you find a good spot. Let the birds come to you rather than chasing them around. Fruiting and flowering trees are good places at which to wait.

Watching birds in forests is quite a skill. It is easy to crash noisily through the undergrowth without seeing a single bird. Use the edge of the forest or large trails through forest where you can move quickly and quietly and have a good view into the canopy. An excellent chance to get good views is where a road runs through montane forest or scrub. Walk quietly along the road, stopping at intervals for a few minutes. Many birds will fly across the road and you will get good side views into the upper canopy on the downhill side.

Three methods are regularly used to attract forest birds for better viewing, or even for photography. One way is called 'pishing'. This consists of sucking air sharply through compressed lips to make squeaky noises similar to the distress calls of some species. Many babblers, bulbuls, tits and other birds will come close to investigate such sounds. A similar result can be achieved by imitating the calls of small owls. In much of southern China, the calls of the Barred Owlet, *poop poo poop poop*, will attract an excited flock of small birds. The third technique involves use of a small tape recorder with a playback speaker. Playback of the calls of birds will often attract them to within close range. This can however, cause disturbance to breeding birds and caution should be exercised.

Where to find birds in China?

With such a vast country, the choice is infinite. Almost all of China's 600 nature reserves are interesting for the bird enthusiast, but we can help narrow down the possibilities with a brief review of the special species and special places in each of the seven main regions of China. The accompanying map marks 40 of the prime sites for birdwatchers and shows the dimensions used to identify the seven biogeographical areas of China.

In the north-east of the country one can find some wetland sites that are important for breeding waterfowl. Oriental Storks, several species of crane and many ducks, geese and swans breed in these areas. Best localities are Zhalong and Momoge, but Lake Kankha on the Russian border is also a wonderful place. These areas should be visited in summer. Forest birds are best seen in Changbaishan reserve or, for the real tundra birds such as Capercaillie and Hazel Grouse, up in the conifer forests north of Harbin and the Huzhong-Hanma reserve.

For the birds of the great northern steppes, you should travel up the Yellow River through the loess and ordos plateaux to Helanshan and Qilianshan mountains and the Xilingele reserve of Inner Mongolia. Other excellent places in northern China include Beidaihe on the Hebei coast, a great place to watch passage migrants, whilst the mountain reserves of Shennongjia in Hubei and several reserves in the Qinling mountains just south of Xian in Shaanxi are excellent places to visit.

In the north-west of China, the two mountain ranges of Tianshan and Altay provide a range of habitats, from alpine and conifer forests to desert conditions. There are some important lakes in Tianshan where geese, swans and some cranes nest. Desert birds can be seen in the Tarim and Turpan depressions, but travel is difficult from the main town of Urumqi. The great reserve of Arjin mountains has salt lakes and mountains and is about as remote as you can get in China.

The plateau region of China is full of potential, but most birdwatchers do not get far from Lhasa. You can travel down into the Chumbi valley between Sikkim and Bhutan to see wetland birds and some Himalayan birds, or down into the Yalong Zangpo (Brahmaputra) valley and the moist forests of south-eastern Tibet.

In south-western China you can find the bulk of the country's narrow-ranging endemic birds in Sichuan: in the Wolong panda reserve or Emeishan sacred mountain reserve. Wolong in the Qionglai mountains boasts nine different species of pheasant. Fanjingshan in Guizhou province and Baimaxueshan in Yunnan are other excellent reserves to visit in this unit.

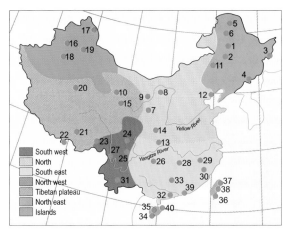

1 Zhalong	16 Tianshan	28 Dongting Lake
2 Momoge	17 Altayshan	29 Poyang Lake
3 Lake Kankha	18 Tarim Basin	30 Wuyishan
4 Changbaishan	19 Turpan	31 Xishuangbanna
5 Huzhong	Depression	32 Dinghushan
6 Hanma	20 Arjin	33 Babaoshan
7 Loess Plateau	Mountains	34 Jianfengling
8 Ordos Plateau	21 Lhasa	35 Bawangling
9 Helanshan	22 Chumbi	36 Kenting
10 Qilianshan	Valley	37 Tailuge
11 Xilingele	23 Yalong Zangpo	(Taroko)
12 Beidaihe	Valley, Medog	38 Dawushan
13 Shennongjia	24 Wolong	39 Taipokau
14 Qinling	25 Emeishan	Maipo
Mountains	26 Fanjingshan	40 Dongzhaigang
15 Qinghai Lake	27 Baimaxueshan	

South-eastern China contains important lakes such as Dongting and Poyang in the Yangtze valley, where hundreds of thousands of waterbirds winter, including White Cranes, swans, geese and storks. Visitors should take plenty of clothes in winter and a snorkel in summer. The endemic mountain birds of the south-east are best seen in Wuyishan reserve in Fujian and Jiangxi provinces, where excellent conditions have been provided for foreigners.

Tropical south China has many good places to see birds. Most famous are Xishuangbanna in the tropics of south Yunnan, Dinghushan and Babaoshan in Guangdong province, Jianfengling and Bawangling on Hainan island, and such excellent reserves as Kenting, Taroko and Dawushan in Taiwan. For forest birds in Hong Kong the visitor should go to Taipokau, whilst for waders and waterbirds one should visit Maipo marshes reserve in Hong Kong or Dongzhaigang on Hainan.

Little Grebe *Tachybaptus ruficollis* 25cm

Small buoyant grebe of reedy lakes and estuaries. Breeding adults have black forehead and crown with chestnut sides of head and front of neck. Eye is dark and base of bill has fleshy yellow gape spot. Winter and juvenile plumage is paler and more uniform, with gape spot less conspicuous. Breeding birds utter shrill trill and make skittish runs over water. Lacks any white on wing, but trailing edge pale. Dives for prolonged periods under surface. The nest is made on floating heap of vegetation; eggs are covered with debris when parents are absent. Widespread and common over much of China.

Great Crested Grebe *Podiceps cristatus* 50cm

Larger, elegant grebe with slender neck and pronounced dark crest. Underparts whitish; upperparts uniform greyish-brown. In breeding season, adults have chestnut nape and manelike 'ear' tufts. Distinguished from Red-necked Grebe by white on side of face extending over eye and by longer bill. In breeding season pairs perform elaborate courtship dance, facing each other, rising tall and nodding heads together, sometimes carrying vegetation in bill. Adults have deep resonant call. Young beg with piping *ping–ping*. Locally common and widespread on larger lakes. Partly migratory.

Great Cormorant *Phalacrocorax carbo* 85cm

Large blackish cormorant with buffy-white patch around throat. Plumage mostly glossy greenish-black; wing feathers edged black. In breeding season there is a small white patch on flanks and the sides of the head are decorated with whitish plumes. There is a ridge of stiff black feathers down back of nape. Bill and bare skin yellowish. Juveniles have whitish underparts. Cormorants breed on islets off the east coast and migrate south in winter. These birds are used by Chinese fishermen to catch fish. Formerly common but now greatly reduced in numbers. A large wintering flock has developed in Hong Kong.

Great White Pelican *Pelecanus onocrotalus* 165cm

Huge pinkish-white rare pelican with bluish bill with pink edges and pink feet. Distinguished from Spot-billed Pelican by larger size and whiter plumage, and from both Spot-billed and Dalmatian Pelicans by a tuft of long narrow feathers springing from the back of the head and feathers of forehead extending in a point over the culmen. Eyes are red. The wing in flight has more black than Dalmatian Pelican's. Lives in small flocks, summering and probably breeding on lakes in north-west Xinjiang and the upper Yellow River but wintering to south-east China on large rivers, estuaries and along the coast.

Dalmatian Pelican *Pelecanus crispus* 175cm

Huge pelican with greyish-white plumage, pale yellow eyes, orange or yellow gular pouch. Underwing is white, with only tips of flight feathers black (Eastern White Pelican has more black in wing). Nape has curly crest. Feathers across forehead do not protrude forward as on Eastern White Pelican, but form crescentic line. Bill is grey, edged pink. Skin around eye is pinkish. Feet greyish-black. Gregarious and fishes in groups. Rare and local in northern China, migrating to winter in the south. A few regularly winter in Hong Kong.

Black-crowned Night-heron *Nycticorax nycticorax* 61cm

Elegant black, white and grey heron with scarlet eyes and short legs. Adult has black cap and back, grey flight feathers and whitish underparts. Two long slender white plumes trail from nape. Immature is streaky brown, spotted with white. Birds are largely nocturnal, spending the day at colonial roosts. At dusk they fly out to feed in neighbouring rice fields, marshes, mangroves or open areas. The call is a characteristic harsh *kowak–kowak*. The species is widespread but local, generally holding its own in most localities. It is locally migratory.

Cattle Egret *Bubulcus ibis* 50cm

Small, chunky white egret with stout yellow bill and blackish legs. The lower mandible is well feathered, producing jowl-like impression. In breeding season birds lack any plumes, but are easily distinguished by golden staining on crested crown, breast and lower back. In breeding season legs may be yellowish and bill orange. Cattle Egrets are gregarious, and differ from other egrets in feeding mostly on dry ground generally close to domestic animals, which they frequently ride. Call is low, nasal croak. Roosts with other egrets at night. Widespread and locally common.

Chinese Pond-heron *Ardeola bacchus* 46cm

Small, squat heron with black-tipped yellow bill and yellow legs. Non-breeding adults and juveniles are streaky brown, with white wings noticeable only in flight. Breeding adults are strikingly coloured with the back grey and decorated with short plumes, underparts and throat clean white and head and neck rich chestnut, becoming almost violet on breast. Bare facial skin is greenish-yellow. In flight, the white wings and tail contrast sharply against dark back and neck. Nests communally with other herons. Common and widespread in rice fields and marshes over much of the country, but getting rarer.

17

Great Egret *Casmerodius alba* 90cm

Very large all-white heron with characteristic kink in S-shaped neck. Gape extends far beyond eyes. Winter birds have heavy yellow bill, greenish facial skin and black legs. Breeding adults have barbed plumes on lower back but lack head plumes; have blackish-yellow bill and reddish-pink upper leg. Wingbeats are slow and laboured like a heron's, and feet extend further beyond tail than on other egrets. Less gregarious than other egrets. Call is deep rolling *krr–rr–rra*. Widespread on lakes, marshes, estuaries and coasts, but rarely numerous.

Intermediate Egret *Mesopoyx intermedia* 70cm

Medium-sized, all-white egret. In breeding season has a slight crest and a train of fine, barbed plumes extending from upper back well beyond the tail; also slight plumes on breast. The bill, legs and toes are black. Facial skin greenish-yellow. In winter the egret loses its plumes and the bill is yellow with a black tip. This species is rarer than the Great or Little Egrets and is found mostly in south-east China; visitors occasionally reach Hainan, Taiwan and Hong Kong. Keeps to swampy areas, rice fields, mangroves and coastal mudflats.

Little Egret *Egretta garzetta* 60cm

All-white, smallish egret with slender black bill, black legs and conspicuous yellow feet (Taiwan race has black feet). In breeding plumage the adults have two long plumes on the head and fluffy plumes on back and lower neck. Back plumes are recurved and shorter than on Plumed Egret. Facial skin is yellowish in winter and pinkish in breeding season. Juveniles have brownish bill and feet. Gregarious bird of lakes, estuaries, beaches and rice fields. Widespread and relatively common in suitable habitat, but becoming rarer.

Grey Heron *Ardea cinerea* 95cm

Large grey and white heron with yellow legs and bill. Adult has black browline with two slender plumes, black edge of wing and double row of black spots down front of neck. In flight, black flight feathers contrast with white carpal patch and grey back and wing-coverts. Immature birds are greyer and less patterned than adults. Distinguished from Purple Heron by lack of red or brown in plumage. Flight is slow and ponderous but powerful. Widespread in wetland areas along rivers, lakes, coastline and marshes. Migrates to form large flocks in winter along southern coasts and on Hainan.

Painted Stork *Mycteria leucocephala* 100cm

Whitish stork with black band across breast, black and white wings, black tail and yellow decurved bill. Bare skin on head reddish. In breeding season the back plumage is tinged pink. In flight, black wings have broad white band on greater upper coverts and wing lining and narrow white bands on other upper coverts. Immature is brown with black wings and white rump and vent. It is resident probably only in south-east Tibet.

Oriental Stork *Ciconia boyciana* 105cm

Large, pure white stork with black wings and heavy, straight black bill. Legs are red and bare orbital skin is pink. In flight, black primaries and secondaries contrast sharply against otherwise white plumage. Distinguished from Eurasian White Stork by black instead of reddish bill. Immature is dirty yellowish-white. Breeds in north-east China and inhabits open country and forest. Winters in lakes of lower Yangtze valley, with occasional birds wintering as far south as Hong Kong. Listed as an endangered species.

Oriental White Ibis *Threskiornis melanocephalus* 76cm

Unmistakable hunched white ibis with black legs, black naked head and sharply decurved bill. In breeding season long grey plumes overhang tail and, in flight, a red line of bare skin shows on underwing. Immature is like adult, but head and neck are grey and the head is feathered. Feeds by probing in ponds, marshes and flooded muddy areas. Breeds in north-east China. Wintering birds are seen in south-east China and in tropical regions of south-east Tibet, south Yunnan, Hong Kong and Hainan. Numbers appear to be declining.

Eurasian Spoonbill *Platalea leucorodia* 84cm

Tall white ibis with characteristic black spatulate bill. Legs are dark grey. In breeding season the spatula is yellowish, and there is a yellowish crest. Distinguished from Black-faced Spoonbill by yellow on bill, feathered browline extending further down on bill, and facial skin yellow (not black). Feeds with sideways-sweeping motion of bill in shallow ponds, lakes and estuaries. Flies with fast shallow wingbeats and neck extended. Only sounds are coughs and bill-clapping. Breeds in north of country, and winters in south-east in small flocks.

Lesser Whistling-duck *Dendrocygna javanica* 40cm

Rather long-legged, upright-standing rufous duck. Sexes are alike, with dark brown crown, nape and upperparts and paler rufous underparts. Feathers of back and wing-coverts are scalloped with rufous edges. Undertail-coverts are white. Bill and legs are grey. Immature birds are duller. This duck is partly nocturnal, and gives characteristic musical whistling calls as flocks come down to feed at dusk in rice fields or open wet areas. The nest is made in a tree hole. Resident in southern China, but becoming quite rare. Common in Indochina.

Mute Swan *Cygnus olor* 150cm

Elegant swan with orange bill and characteristic black knob at base of forehead. Holds neck in graceful S-shape while swimming and often holds wings in high arched posture. Young are grey or dirty white with grey-mauve bill. Adult is aggressive in defence of nesting area. Nest is made on pile of reeds. Flies with powerful slow beats and loud whooshing wing noise. Despite name, it hisses in threat and emits deep explosive *heeorr* call. In winter gathers in large flocks on lakes or sea coasts. Breeds on a few northern lakes, with occasional wintering birds reaching southern China.

Tundra Swan *Cygnus columbianus* 142cm

Tall swan with black bill, but much less extensive yellow on bill base and more red may be visible on lower mandible. Yellow on side of upper mandible does not form a forward point. Smaller than Whooper Swan, with which it can easily be confused. Calls are similar to Whooper's but higher-pitched. Groups chorus with crane-like drawn-out *klah* notes. Flocks fly in V-formation. Breeds in Siberian tundra, but migrates in winter through north-east China to lakes in Yangtze valley, where it is much more common than Whooper Swan.

Whooper Swan *Cygnus cygnus* 155cm

Tall swan with black bill and extensive yellow basal area. The yellow extends along the side of the upper mandible to form a point. While swimming, the neck is held straighter than on Mute Swan. Immature is more uniformly coloured than young Mute Swan, and has paler bill. Much larger than Tundra Swan. Breeds at reedbeds in northern lakes, but flocks migrate south in winter. Flight call is characteristic *klo–klo–klo*, but contact call is a loud melancholy bugle-like call. Much quieter wingbeats than Mute Swan's. Generally much rarer than Tundra Swan.

23

Swan Goose *Anser cygnoides* 80cm

Large long-necked goose with rather long black bill forming straight line with forehead and narrow white line around base of bill. Upperparts ashy-brown with feathers edged buff. Foreneck white, crown and back of neck reddish-brown. Sharp contrast between front and back of neck. Legs pink and vent whitish. Flight feathers black. Distinguished from Lesser and Greater White-fronted Geese by black bill, less white on forehead and white front of neck. This goose breeds in north-east China, but winters across the west of China to the lower Yangtze.

Greylag Goose *Anser anser* 76cm

Large grey-brown goose with pink bill and feet. There is no white at base of bill. Feathers of upperparts are grey with white edges, giving the bird a scalloped pattern. The breast is pale ashy-brown and uppertail- and undertail-coverts are white. In flight, the pale forewing contrasts with dark flight feathers. The call of the Greylag is a deep honking. Inhabits steppes, moors and lakes; breeding across north China and wintering on lakes of southern and central China in large flocks. Birds feed on short grasslands and agricultural fields.

Bar-headed Goose *Anser indicus* 70cm

 Smallish goose with diagnostic head pattern of white crown with two black transverse bars on back of head. White of throat extends in a bar down side of neck. Young birds lack black patterning, which is instead light grey. Bill is yellow with black tip and legs are orange. In flight, the bird has uniformly pale upperparts, with only narrow trailing edge of wings dark. Underparts largely white. Breeds on marshes and highland moors of extreme northern China and Tibet and migrates in winter to central China and southern Tibet.

Ruddy Shelduck *Tadorna ferruginea* 63cm

 Orange-chestnut duck with buff head. Shape is rather goose-like. Male in summer has narrow black collar. In flight, the white wing-coverts are conspicuous and speculum is bronze-green. Bill and legs are black. Nests in holes in the banks of small streams. Keeps to inland lakes and rivers; rarely visits the coast. Feeds on a wide range of fish and invertebrates, as well as some plants. This is a hardy bird, breeding in the extreme north-east and north-west of China and Tibet up to 4,600m, but migrating for the winter to south and central China.

Common Shelduck *Tadorna tadorna* 60cm

Very strikingly patterned black and white duck with glossy greenish-black head contrasting sharply with bright red bill and pronounced knob at base of forehead. There is a cinnamon band across the forepart of the body. Female is similar to male but slightly duller, and with small or no bill knob. Juvenile is mottled brown, with dull red bill and white patch on side of face. Breeds in holes in banks of salty or brackish lakes and rarely freshwater lakes in north and north-east China, but migrates in winter to south-east China, where it is quite common.

Mandarin Duck *Aix galericulata* 40cm

The classic Chinese duck celebrated in paintings through the centuries. An amazingly decorative male, with sweeping bold white brow, golden mane of hackles and extraordinary cinnamon display 'sails' that are held erect, concealing wings. Female is less ostentatious: smart grey with elegant white eye-ring and rear eye-stripe. In eclipse plumage male resembles female, but has red instead of grey bill. Breeds in tree holes and lives on wooded streams in north-east China, but migrates to south-east China in winter. Widely recorded but generally rare. Commonly kept in captivity.

Comb Duck *Sarkidiornis melanotos* 76cm

Male (above); female (below)

Male is unmistakable by its large size, black and white coloration and prominent black fleshy comb above bill. White head and neck are finely spotted black; black upperparts are glossed with metallic green and bronze. Female is like male but much smaller, and lacks comb. These ducks nest in natural tree holes and live on wooded pools and rivers. This spectacular species has a large world distribution, but in China it is confined to south-east Tibet and extreme south Yunnan, where it is becoming rare. Stragglers sometimes found in south-east China.

Falcated Duck *Anas falcata* 50cm

Male is quite distinctive, with chestnut crown, shiny sweeping green side of head extending into long drooping nuchal crest and long-plumed black and white tertials. White throat and spot at base of bill distinguish it from much smaller Common Teal. Female is dull brown and difficult to identify at long range unless with male; female has bronzy-brown speculum. Breeds on lakes and wetlands of north-east China, but migrates in winter over much of the country. Regularly winters in Hong Kong. Hunted for its decorative plumes.

27

Baikal Teal *Anas formosa* 42cm

Male is decorative, with black crown and characteristic white crescentic patches on face, patterned with glossy green. Breast is spotted, with rufous wash, and flanks are scaled as on Common Teal; scapulars are elongated, with black centre and white upper edge. Speculum is bronze-green and vent is black. Female is like Garganey and Common Teal but larger, and with white spot at base of bill.

Breeds on Lake Baikal, other parts of Russia and north-east China. Winters in fair numbers on ponds and small lakes in wooded areas over parts of central and southern China, including Hong Kong.

Common Teal *Anas crecca* 42 cm

Small duck with dark green speculum bordered with white. Female is dull mottled brown, but male has buff-bordered iridescent green bar through eye contrasting with rich cinnamon head and grey flanks. Has long white stripe on scapulars. Both sexes have distinctive whitish underparts in flight. Teals also have faster wingbeats than other ducks and travel at great speed. Male has curious cricket-like *kirrip* call. Female replies with thin high *guck*. Common on ponds and marshes in north-west and north-east China, migrating in large flocks to winter in south and east China and along the coast. Large numbers visit Hong Kong.

Mallard *Anas platyrhynchos* 58cm

Unmistakable, familiar male has yellow bill, glossy green head, white neck ring and deep chestnut breast. At distance the pale grey side panel contrasts with dark head, breast and tail. Speculum is blue; tail is curly. Female and young are dowdy streaked brown, with orange blotches on bill. Voice is familiar deep *quack quack*. Flight is fast and wingbeats whistle. Domestic Mallards and Mallard × Spotbill hybrids also occur. This is a widespread and common duck of lakes, ponds, rivers and mangroves. Breeds in northern Asia but winters over much of China.

Spotbill Duck *Anas poecilorhyncha* 60cm

Dark brown duck with pale head, dark crown and eye-stripe and diagnostic yellow-tipped black bill. Throat and cheeks are buffy. Plumage heavily scalloped with pale-edged dark feathers. Speculum is bluish or greenish-purple, usually with white band on trailing edge. Feet are coral-red. White tertials sometimes visible at rest and diagnostic in flight. Sexes are alike, but female is duller. Call is *quack* like domestic duck's. This species inhabits lakes, rivers and coastal mangroves and lagoons. Resident, widespread and quite common in China, though some seasonal movements occur.

Northern Pintail *Anas acuta* 71cm

Elegant, slim, long-necked duck. Male is unmistakable, with brown head, grey-sided bill and very long pointed tail. The white breast extends as a line up side of neck, and there is a conspicuous white panel on rear flank. Speculum is brown with white rear edge. Female and young are brown, with scalloped pattern of pale feather edges; chin and throat are whitish, bill grey. Male's call is short whistled *kree*. Lives on lakes, marshes and coastal estuaries and lagoons. Often upends when feeding. Breeds in northern Asia, but winters in southern China in quite large numbers.

Northern Shoveler *Anas clypeata* 50cm

Unmistakable, with long, broad spatulate bill longer than head. Male has dark green head glossed purple, white breast and chestnut side panel; upperparts streaky brown, with long black and white scapular plumes. In flight, shoulder patch is greyish-blue, white tips to greater wing-coverts form white wingbar and speculum is metallic green. Bill is black and feet orange. Female is scalloped dull brown, with same wing pattern in flight; also has darker belly than most female ducks. Breeds in northern China, wintering south in large numbers on muddy lakes, bogs, marshes and mangroves.

Common Pochard *Aythya ferina* 46cm

This is a smart-looking duck with chestnut-red head contrasting with clear black-tipped grey bill and black breast and mantle. Rump is black; back and side appear grey, but at close range they can be seen to be white with fine black vermiculations. In flight, the grey wing band shows little contrast with darker rest of wing. Eye is bright yellow. Female has grey back, but brownish head, breast and tail and buffy ring around eye. Lives on

Male (above); female (below)

ponds and lakes with abundant water vegetation. Breeds in northwest China, but migrates in winter to east and south China.

Tufted Duck *Aythya fuligula* 43cm

Small compact diving duck with squarish head. Male is black with white side panel. Female is dark brown with some white around base of bill. Both sexes have long recumbent tuft at back of head, bright yellow eye and stout grey bill. Male has purplish gloss to head and is dark blackish-brown on back; distinguished from Scaup by tuft and blacker back. In eclipse plumage the tuft is lost. Swims buoyantly and makes regular deep dives to feed. Breeds in north-east China, but winters over most of country on lakes, reeded ponds and occasionally on sea coast. Relatively common.

Smew *Mergellus albellus* 40cm

Small, elegant duck. Breeding male is white with black mask, nape stripe, mantle, primaries and pattern of narrow lines at side of breast; sides of body finely vermiculated with grey lines. Female and immature male are grey above with two white wingbars, white underparts, blackish ocular region and chestnut forehead, crown and nape; distinguished from mergansers by white cheeks. Smews live in the tundra areas of northern China on small ponds and rivers, breeding in tree holes. In winter they migrate south over much of country. Widespread but generally rare.

Red-breasted Merganser *Mergus serrator* 56cm

Male is black and white duck with long narrow reddish bill and hooked tip. Black head has shaggy crest. Flanks are patterned with characteristic white feathers edged and shafted black which give a scaly pattern. Feet are red. Distinguished from Scaly-sided Merganser by rufous on breast streaked dark and from Goosander by breast and longer crest. Female and non-breeding male duller and brown with reddish head grading gradually into whitish throat. Breeds in northeast but winters along coasts and bays of east and southern China. This is a frequent bird that inhabits lakes and wooded streams swimming low in water and diving with ease. Generally breeds on the ground.

Black Kite *Milvus migrans* 65cm

Dark brown kite with slightly forked tail. Plumage is all brown, with blackish ear-coverts and black wingtips. Underparts are streaky. In flight, the pale wing patches and vent are visible. These birds are aerial acrobats, riding among thermals or making long buoyant glides; they are at ease among the skyscrapers of Hong Kong. Most food is taken from the water surface and eaten on the wing. This is a common scavenger of estuaries and coastline in eastern and southern China, with occasional migrant birds turning up in south-west China and south-east Tibet; the commonest raptor in Hong Kong. Northern black-eared races sometimes considered a separate species.

Black-winged Kite *Elanus caeruleus* 32cm

Attractive small pale kite with grey upperparts and white underparts contrasting with black shoulders and primaries. Red eye and square-cut, slightly forked tail are distinctive. Glides with wings held in marked 'V'. Often hovers like a kestrel when hunting for mice, snakes and insects. Distinguished from harriers by flight pattern, black shoulders, tail shape and red eye. Rests on prominent tree perch or telephone wires and is rather tame. Frequents open grassy and marshy areas, including rice fields, in southern and eastern China. It appears to be becoming more common and widespread.

Lammergeier *Gypaetus barbatus* 110cm

This is a large yellowish vulture with a black band through the eye contrasting with otherwise whitish head. Underparts are orange-buff and upperparts brown with buff streaks. Has slight beard, and adult has red eye-ring. In flight, the straight, pointed wings and long wedge-shaped tail are diagnostic. This is a bird of high mountains up to 7,000m, found harrying wild sheep and domestic yak herds, waiting for animals to fall and injure themselves or freeze in winter. It carries small prey and bones of larger prey and drops them on to rocks, to help break them for easier eating.

Himalayan Griffon *Gyps himalayensis* 122cm

Large pale buffy-brown vulture with underparts streaked white. The head and neck are lightly feathered with white down. Has collar of fluffy buff plumes. Primaries are black. Immature is dark brown with streaking from pale feather shafts. Flight appears in very slow motion. Has long, upturned 'fingers' at wingtips, with wings held just above horizontal. Usually seen soaring, sometimes in small parties, or roosting among rocky crags. Gives occasional clucking and whistling sounds. This is a common scavenger in some parts of the Himalayas, Tibet plateau and west and central China in open high-altitude habitats.

Northern Goshawk *Accipiter gentilis* 56cm

Adult (left); juvenile (right)

Large, powerful hawk without crest or mesial throat stripe and with distinctive broad white eyebrow. Underparts of adult are white, finely barred pinkish-brown; upperparts uniform grey. Juvenile is browner, with pale feather edges giving scaly pattern to upperparts and having bold black streaking on underparts. Bright gleaming eye varies from yellow in juvenile to deep red in older age. It is a hawk of woodlands, able to twist and turn fast on its broad, rounded wings. It preys largely on pigeons, but can also take gamebirds and smallish mammals. A fairly common bird in temperate and subalpine forests.

Greater Spotted Eagle *Aquila clanga* 70cm

Adult (left); in flight (right)

Uniform dark brown eagle with short tail and yellow cere and feet. Plumage colour and pattern vary with age. Juvenile has conspicuous white spots and bars on upperwings and back. All plumages show white U-shape on upper-tail-coverts in flight. Tail much shorter than on Golden or Imperial Eagles. Inhabits open swampy areas near lakes and marshes, or open areas during migration. Feeds mostly on frogs, snakes, fish and birds. Breeds across northern China, wintering in south of the country and through to Indonesia. Never common, but rather regular.

Golden Eagle *Aquila chrysaetos* 85cm

Adult (left); in flight (right)

Large rich brown eagle with golden-naped head, and in flight often shows some conspicuous white at base of tail. Bill is massive. In flight, distinguished by long, evenly rounded tail, wings held in shallow 'V'. Separated from Imperial by lack of white on scapulars. Immature is distinctive, with white wing patches and white base of tail. Lives in rugged steppes and mountains with cliffs and open country, where it feeds on gamebirds, marmots and other mammals. Soars majestically on thermals. This is a widespread but uncommon bird over much of the country and up to high altitudes in the Himalayas.

Common Kestrel *Falco tinnunculus* 35cm

Small, delicate falcon. Male has bluish-grey head and tail and vinaceous rufous-brown back, spotted with black. There is a black moustachial line below eye, and the tail has a black subterminal bar and white tip. Female and young are much browner and more strongly barred. Underparts buff with dark streaks. Eye is dark and cere and feet bright yellow; bill is slaty. The Common Kestrel regularly hovers whilst searching for prey, and nests on cliffs, building ledges and in trees. The call is a plaintive *yek–yek–yek*. This is a widespread and common falcon of open areas and short grasslands.

Peregrine Falcon *Falco peregrinus* 46cm

Large, powerful, sleek falcon with steely-grey upperparts, finely barred underparts, and characteristic blackish head markings with pronounced moustachial line extending below eye. Cere and feet bright yellow and bill slaty. Juvenile is browner than adult and has streaked underparts. In flight, the broad-based pointed wings give the bird a characteristic 'anchor' shape. Flies with powerful short strokes interspersed with glides, often up to great height. Stoops on prey such as pigeons at great speed, striking prey in mid-air. Inhabits rocky mountainous and wide open areas. Widespread but generally rare.

Chukar *Alectoris chukar* 38cm

Boldly marked partridge with white throat and lower face, bordered by black band which runs through eye and across lower throat and contrasts with bright red bill and fleshy eye-ring. Upperparts are pinkish-grey and breast is orange-buff. Flanks are beautifully barred with black, chestnut and white stripes. Feet are pink. Lives in pairs or coveys in open mountainous areas, high plateaux, steppes and dry grassland. There are several races. Desert birds are palest. Widespread in north and west China and locally common.

37

Blue-breasted Quail *Coturnix chinensis* 14cm

Male is an unmistakable tiny gamebird with bold black and white pattern on throat. Breast, flank, rump, forecrown and stripe through eye blue-grey. Upperparts otherwise rich olive-brown, barred black and streaked white. Vent and centre of abdomen dark chestnut. Female is reddish-brown above, mottled with black and streaked white; abdomen is buff, finely barred with black. Female is easily confused with buttonquails. Iris is reddish and feet are yellow. Call is a sweet double whistle, *ti–yu, ti–yu*. A common flocking bird in lowland grassy areas, scrub and rice stubble in south and east China.

Satyr Tragopan *Tragopan satyra* 70cm

Beautiful crimson tragopan with black head and throat. Crest is black, tipped red. Plumage is mostly decorated with circular white or pearl dots outlined with black. Wings and tail bluish, barred with buff. 'Horns' and lappets blue, revealing green and red patches when extended by displaying male. Similar to more widespread Temminck's Tragopan, but more crimson and lacks scaled pattern on underparts. Female is duller and mottled black and rufous-brown; orbital skin bluish. Lives in rhododendron forests in a narrow range of south-east Tibet between 2,300 and 4,000m, but coming lower in winter.

Silver Pheasant *Lophura nyctemera* 94cm

Male unmistakable, with long white tail, white back, black crown and full long black crest. Central tail feathers are pure white; other feathers of back and tail are finely barred and patterned black. Underparts are black. The bare facial skin and feet are bright red. The female is olive-brown to chestnut above, and brown, streaked and mottled with white or buff below; she also has dark crest and red facial skin and feet. Male gives harsh piercing calls. The species is common in evergreen forest, bamboo thickets and scrub at moderate altitudes over much of southern and eastern China.

Swinhoe's Pheasant *Lophura swinhoei* 81cm

Male is a long-legged pheasant with crest, white patch on back and long white central feathers contrasting with otherwise purplish-black tail. Head, neck and underparts bluish-black; rump is black, scalloped with shimmering green edges. Bare facial area and legs are red. Female has dark brown upperparts with fine black vermiculations and streaked orange; underparts are cinnamon with black barring. This is a very rare endemic of the central mountains of Taiwan at 800–1,500m. The population was rescued by captive-breeding and is being built up by reintroductions.

39

Blue Eared-pheasant *Crossoptilon auritum* 90cm

Bluish-grey pheasant with black velvety cap, scarlet bare orbital area and long white 'ear' tufts. There is a whitish bar behind nape. The tail is arched and central feathers are grey and filamentous, contrasting with purplish-blue outer feathers. Like other eared-pheasants, lives in small parties in open alpine meadows and juniper-rhododendron scrub at high altitudes, the different species being allopatric. This species is the most north-westerly in distribution, ranging from north-central China to north Sichuan. White Eared-pheasant to south is much whiter, with shorter 'ears'.

Reeve's Pheasant *Syrmaticus reevesii* 180cm

Male is unmistakable with its extraordinarily long, barred tail (up to 1.5m). Head is boldly patterned black and white. Upperparts are golden-yellow scaled with black feather edges; centre of belly and thighs are black. Female is mottled reddish-brown, with scaled breast and much shorter tail. This is a rather rare inhabitant of north-east and central China, living in wooded hills at 300–1,600m in steep valleys and canyons of deciduous oak forest and mixed conifers. The long tail feathers are commonly used in the flamboyant headdresses of Beijing Opera.

Elliot's Pheasant *Syrmaticus ellioti* 81cm

Male is brownish with a pointed, elongated brown tail barred with silvery-grey. The bird is patterned with white sides of neck, wing bars, abdomen and vent. Bare facial skin is scarlet. Rump is black, scalloped with narrow white edges. Similar to Hume's Pheasant, but distinguished by white on side of neck. Female has reddish-brown crown with grey nape and mantle. Upperparts are mottled and vermiculated chestnut, grey and black, throat and foreneck are black and rest of underparts are white with cinnamon barring. This is an uncommon bird in forested hills of south-east China.

Mikado Pheasant *Syrmaticus mikado* 86cm

Male is an elegant blackish, long-tailed pheasant with distinct glossy purple-blue edges to feathers of mantle, breast and rump, forming conspicuous scalloped pattern against sooty-black feather centres. Pointed tail is barred black and mottled white. Wings are black with a conspicuous white bar and white tips to secondaries and tertials. Bare orbital skin is crimson. Female is mottled grey below, and brown above with mottling of reddish and black with white streaks. This is a rare endemic resident of the central mountains of Taiwan at 1,800–3,000m.

41

Common Pheasant *Phasianus colchicus* 85cm

The familiar pheasant of Europe and North America originates in China. Male has glossy black head with prominent 'ear tufts' and broad fleshy red orbital skin. Some races have white neck ring. Body is gloriously coloured, with shimmering decorative feathers ranging from dark green to copper to gold; wings greyish, and tail is elongated, pointed and brown with black bands. Much smaller female is banded pale brown. Male's call is two-note explosive hacking followed by whirr of wings. Widespread in scrubby open areas.

Golden Pheasant *Chrysolophus pictus* 98cm

Male is dazzling with golden-plumed crown and back, gold and black barred nape ruff, metallic green mantle and crimson underparts. Wing is metallic blue; tail is elongated, arched, and central feathers are blackish with small buff spots. Smaller female is buffy-brown, finely banded with black, above, and paler buff below. It is confined to south and central China, where it is quite common in scrubby montane forest and bamboo at moderate altitudes. Keeps to dense thickets, descending into open fields in winter. Often kept in captivity.

Lady Amherst's Pheasant *Chrysolophus amherstiae* 150cm

The male has a glossy dark green crown, throat and upper breast, short scarlet crest and white mane scalloped with black edges. Back and wings are glossy dark green and belly is white. Rump is yellow, and long tail slightly arched with white feathers narrowly banded black. Several orange-tipped elongated tail-coverts. Female upperparts barred black and cinnamon, with white throat and chestnut breast finely edged black; flanks and undertail-coverts buff, barred black. An uncommon bird of forested hills from south-east Tibet through Yunnan to Guizhou.

Grey Peacock Pheasant *Polyplectron bicalcaratum* 53cm

Unmistakable gamebird, with barred and peppered dark brownish-grey plumage spotted on mantle and tail with metallic violet eyespots bordered buffish-white. Throat is whitish and there is a slight bushy crest. Female is smaller and duller, with black ocelli edged buffish-whitish. The voice is a loud, far-carrying double note, *taa–pwi*, and curious warbling calls. This is a widespread bird through dense evergreen lowland and submontane forests of the Himalayas, south-west China and Hainan, but it is generally not numerous.

43

Green Peafowl *Pavo muticus* 350cm

Unmistakable huge green pheasant with long tail and vertical tuft of feathers on top of head. Ocellated tail of male is generally held as long train, but is fanned out and shaken in display. Male has glossy green neck and mantle and diagnostic blue and yellow bare skin on face. In flight, appears dark with cinnamon primaries. Female is smaller, more dowdy, and has much shorter tail. Feeds on the ground but roosts in trees. Gives loud trumpeting calls, *kay–yaw, kay–yaw*, often from roost perch. This is now a rare bird confined to a few localities in south Yunnan and possibly south-east Tibet.

White-breasted Waterhen *Amaurornis phoenicurus* 33cm

Distinctive large rail with slaty-grey upperparts, white face, throat and breast and chestnut belly and vent. Legs and bill are yellow, base of bill sometimes red. Juveniles are dull brown below. The calls are remarkable, with a monotonous *kee–wak, kee–wak*, often at night, and loud cacophonous group calls. The birds nest in bushes close to water. Swims well. This is a common but rather shy and retiring bird of wet open areas and the edge of paddy fields. The waterhen is widespread in southern China, and partly migratory. Birds are frequently caught for food.

Common Moorhen *Gallinula chloropus* 33cm

Distinctive large aquatic rail with black plumage, white of undertail pattern accentuated by constant flicking and cocking of tail, and red horny frontal comb with yellow-tipped red bill. Legs are yellowish-green. Underparts are sooty-grey with white side line. Swims with characteristic jerky motion and makes noisy paddling run across water surface prior to flight. The juvenile is dark brownish-grey and lacks red comb. The call is a bubbling *pyurrk* or clucking *kreck, kreck, kreck, kreck*. Common and widespread on ponds, rivers, swamps and mangroves.

Purple Swamphen *Porphyrio porphyrio* 48cm

Chicken-sized purplish-black rail with red legs and red frontal helmet and bill. Bill is very heavy. Distinguished from Common Moorhen by larger size, purplish colour, red bill tip and lower legs, lack of black centre to undertail-coverts and lack of white side stripe. Immature is dowdy. Gives deep tooting calls. Lives in swampy marshes and reedbeds, but comes on to open areas to feed. Generally rather shy, rushing for the cover of reedbeds when seen. This is only a marginal inhabitant of China, occurring in south Yunnan, south-east China and Hainan. Generally rare in China, but common further south.

45

Common Coot *Fulica atra* 38cm

 Unmistakable large black aquatic rail with horny white frontal shield and white bill. Lacks the white tail pattern of Common Moorhen. Juvenile is blackish with white throat and lacks white side line of Common Moorhen. Feeds on aquatic vegetation and nests on heap of floating weed. Dives regularly and swims with head-nodding motion. Runs along water surface prior to flight. The coot gives a variety of nasal explosive calls. A common bird on lakes and mangroves in southern and eastern China. Sometimes forms large flocks, especially in winter, when partly migratory.

Common Crane *Grus grus* 125cm

 Forecrown is black, centre of crown red, and head and neck dark slaty-grey. There is a broad white curved stripe from behind the eye down to back of neck. Plumage otherwise grey with brownish wash on back and elongated bushy tertials. Legs are black, bill is brownish. Has mating dance of high fluttering leaps. Pairs duet with clear far-carrying horn sound. Migrating flocks give trumpeting *krraw*. Favours wetlands, marshes and shallow lakes. Breeds in north-east and north-west China, but migrates south in winter to southern China and Indochina.

Black-naped Crane *Grus nigricollis* 150cm

Tall whitish crane with head, throat and entire neck black except for a white patch below and behind eye. Bare lores and crown are red. Tail, primaries and elongated tertials are black. Legs are black, and bill is black with yellow tip. Call is a series of loud trumpeting honks. Flies like other cranes with neck outstretched and in 'V'-formation. Breeds in north-west and north-central China in swamps and around lakes. Winters in south in wet cultivated areas of Bhutan, south Tibet, Yunnan and Guizhou, where it may be a pest of agricultural crops. This is now a rare bird.

White-naped Crane *Grus vipio* 150cm

Tall grey and white crane with bare red patch on side of face edged and patterned black. Throat and back of neck white. Grey of breast and front of neck extends up side of neck in a narrow pointed line. Primaries are black. Rest of plumage various shades of grey. Bill is yellow and legs are crimson. This splendid crane breeds in north-east and north-west China in marshy swamps and at reedy lakeshores. Birds migrate south in winter to lakes and river banks of the lower Yangtze, with vagrants reaching Taiwan and Fujian.

Red-crowned Crane *Grus japonensis* 150cm

Tall, elegant white rare crane with bare red crown. Lores, cheeks, throat and sides of neck are black. A broad white band extends from ear-coverts down back of neck. Rest of plumage white except for black secondaries and elongated drooping tertials. Dancing display on breeding grounds is much revered in local cultures. Flies with neck extended and in 'V'-formation. Breeds in north-east China, but migrates south to winter in eastern provinces and Yangtze lakes, also to Korea and Japan. Accidental in Taiwan.

Demoiselle Crane *Anthropoides virgo* 105cm

Elegant pale bluish-grey crane with white crown and long white-plumed ear tufts contrasting against blackish head, neck and elongated breast feathers. Elongated tertials are not bushy and overhang tail. Black of breast extends lower down front than on Common Crane. Iris is red in male, orange in female. Call is a trumpeting similar to that of Common Crane, but shriller and flatter. Flies in 'V'-formation with neck extended. A bird of high plateaux, cold deserts and swamps at up to 5,000m. Breeds in north-east and north-west China and winters in southern Tibet.

Black-winged Stilt *Himantopus himantopus* 37cm

Unmistakable extraordinarily long, pale red legs; blackish wings and back with white body and tail. Black bill is straight and slender. Back of head blackish. Female is somewhat browner than male. Flocks feed in shallow pools and fly in dazzling flickering parties. Wing is pointed in flight, and red legs extend far beyond tail. Call is a persistent *klit–klit–klit* similar to that of Pied Avocet; also gives tern-like cries, *kyee*. Breeds in west and central China. Locally common, wintering in coastal lagoons and mangroves of southern and eastern China.

Pied Avocet *Recurvirostra avosetta* 43cm

Unmistakable tall black and white wader with long grey legs and long, slender, markedly upturned black bill. Swishes bill from side to side whilst feeding. Swims well and upends. Flies with fast fluttery wingbeats but makes long glides. From below, looks all white with black wingtips; above, has black wingbar and shoulder stripe. Makes frequent clear flutish calls, *kluit, kluit, kluit*. Adults give 'broken wing' display to distract predators from young. Avocets breed in north China, but gather in large wintering flocks along the south-east coast and through Tibet to India. Accidental in Taiwan.

49

Little Ringed Plover *Charadrius dubius* 16cm

Small plover with brownish-grey upperparts, diagnostic complete white collar and white underparts. In breeding season has black neck-ring and black patterning on face. In winter there is an incomplete brown neck band. Distinguished from other small plovers by lack of white wingbar in flight. Call in flight is drawn-out *peeyoo*. Resident and plentiful along the coast of China with some seasonal movements. Breeding in south-east recently confirmed. Lives in active flocks, running and scampering about on sand- and mudbars searching for insects and crustaceans.

Pacific Golden Plover *Pluvialis fulva* 24cm

Short-legged wader with rounded head, short blunt black bill and heavy hunched body. Legs are grey. Coloration is mottled buff in winter with pale buff band across forehead and down side. Summer plumage is rich golden brown upperparts mottled with black, black underparts from eye to belly separated from golden upperparts by clean white band across forecrown and down sides. Breeds in extreme north of Siberia but migrates south down the China coast in winter. Inhabits coasts and open areas of short cropped grass. Call is a shrill whistle. Runs a short distance before sudden halt. Flies in fast flocks.

Red-wattled Lapwing *Vanellus indicus* 32cm

 Tall, long-legged lapwing with black crown, throat and upper breast contrasting with white side of head. Back is grey and wings are black and white; tail is white with broad black sub-terminal band. Legs are yellow. Bill is red with black tip, and there is a diagnostic red wattle in front of eye. Call is a series of loud screams, *did–he–do–it, pity–to–do–it*. Runs in sudden bursts between standing very still. In flight, reveals extravagant black and white wing pattern. This is a common bird on rocky, sandy river banks, around marshes and occasionally on short grassland and rice stubble.

Northern Lapwing *Vanellus vanellus* 31cm

 Smallish lapwing with black crown and characteristic long, thin, recurved crest. Throat and upper breast are blackish, abdomen white. Upperparts bronzy-green; undertail-coverts cinnamon. Non-breeding birds and juveniles are duller, with more black on side of head; juvenile has white throat. Bold black and white pattern of underparts startling in flight, especially the conspicuous courtship display of male and mobbing flight when disturbed by a predator. Characteristic call is shrill *ee–wit, ee–wit*. Breeds in open areas in north, but migrates south in winter to form large flocks on farmland and open grassy areas.

51

Great Knot *Calidris tenuirostris* 29cm

Chunky, short-legged wader with long straight black bill, white belly, grey upperparts and breast mottled with dark spots. In summer shoulders have bright chestnut spots and the breast has a dark blackish breast band. In flight shows white wing bar and rump. Legs are dark greenish. Voice is a whistled *pyuee*. Winter birds distinguished from smaller Red Knot by longer bill, less pronounced whitish eyebrow and bolder spotting on back and breast. Breeds in Siberia but migrates to southeast China along coasts in winter.

Eastern Curlew *Numenius madagascariensis* 62cm

A large mottled wader with extremely elongated and recurved bill. Distinguished from Eurasian Curlew by dark, rather than white, back, undertail coverts and wing lining. Distinguished from Whimbrel by larger size, longer bill, dark rump and lack of striped crown. The Eastern Curlew breeds in Siberia and northeast China in open boggy habitat but passes through China along coasts and major rivers during winter migrations to Taiwan and southern coasts. Favours large mudflats and sometimes mixes with Eurasian Curlew and has similar rising, plaintive *cur-li* call.

Common Redshank *Tringa totanus* 27cm

Elegant, long-legged wader with distinctive red legs and red base to bill. Summer plumage is mottled brown above and white with brown streaking on breast below. Distinguished from Spotted Redshank by browner colour, streaked breast and lack of black in breeding plumage. Winter plumage is greyer. In flight, has broad white band on trailing edge of inner wing. Voice is musical three-note call, *teu–hu–hu*, with raised first note. Breeds in northern China, wintering in the southeast. This is a common bird of estuaries, mudflats and mangroves.

Common Greenshank *Tringa nebularia* 35cm

Largish grey-brown wader with white tail and triangular patch extending up back, long green legs and long, rather heavy and slightly upturned black bill. In flight, feet extend beyond tail and wing has white lining. At close range, fine black bars can be seen on tail. Browner and darker in summer, greyer in winter, with white underparts. Call is a noisy, loud, ringing *tew* rapidly repeated three or more times. This is a rather uncommon bird breeding in northern latitudes and wintering in the south of the country on mudflats, marshes and sea coasts.

Terek Sandpiper *Xenus cinereus* 23cm

Medium-sized wader with shortish bright yellow legs and long upturned black bill with yellow base. General plumage grey above and white below with dark eyestripe, white supercilium, black primaries and black line along scapular. In flight legs do not extend beyond tail and rear edge of wing is white. In winter the back is grey without black on scapulars. Distinguished from Grey-tailed Tattler by recurved bill and from other waders with recurved bills by short yellow legs. Call is loud rapid shrill whinny. Breeds in Tibet and Qinghai. Passage migrant in winter along southern coasts, Hainan and Yunnan.

Common Sandpiper *Actitis hypoleucos* 20cm

Small, short-legged wader with diagnostic brown patch on side of breast. Wings and tail are barred and mottled, but back is uniform grey-brown. Shows white wingbar during characteristic low flight over water with wings flicked between short glides. Constantly bobs head and tail when walking or standing. Bill and feet are greyish. Voice is a shrill piping *wee–wee–wee–wee*. This is a common and widespread bird along rivers, coasts and the shores of lakes and ponds, generally seen singly or in pairs. Breeds in northern China, but winters in the south and beyond to Indonesia.

Saunders's Gull *Larus saundersi* 33cm

Small gull, distinguished in both black-headed summer plumage and white-headed winter plumage from Common Black-headed Gull by smaller size, shorter neck, black stubby bill, black underside to outer primaries and zebra pattern on folded primaries at rest. Call is a shrill *eek eek*. Very buoyant flight. Often mixes with Common Black-headed Gulls. Breeds in only a few sites on east China coast and winters along the south coast, including Hong Kong. This is a rare and endangered bird, generally seen feeding along the tide-line on crabs and crustaceans.

Common Black-headed Gull *Larus ridibundus* 40cm

Summer plumage of black head with white eye-ring and reddish bill. In winter the head is white with a black spot behind eye. Distinguished from Great Black-headed by smaller size and lack of yellow on bill; from Saunders's Gull by larger size, bill colour and wingtip pattern; from Relict Gull by wingtip pattern; and from Brown-headed Gull by dark eyes and wingtip pattern. Call is a rolling, screaming *krreeay*. This is a common bird along the coast of China and on many inland lakes. Large flocks gather around favoured wintering grounds such as parks in Kunming town.

55

Brown-headed Gull *Larus brunnicephalus* 44cm

Slightly larger than Black-headed Gull but summer brown head much paler brown with only near edge dark. Bill longer and red. Has large white patches near tips of black primaries. In winter plumage dark of head reduced to patch on ear coverts, spot in front of eye and some grey on crown. Immature has black-tipped yellow bill and black tip to tail. Breeds in northeast and western China and on Qinghai Lake. Winters in west Yunnan and southeast Tibet.

Slaty-backed Gull *Larus schistisagus* 61cm

Large gull with dark grey mantle, yellow bill and red spot near tip of lower mandible. Head is white in summer or streaked with brown in winter. Immature is mottled brown with black terminal tail bar and some white at base of tail. Subadult is like adult with brown streaks on neck and black spot in front of red spot on bill. Legs are pink. Adult is distinguished from pink legged races of Herring Gull by much darker mantle. Immature cannot be distinguished from Herring Gull in field. Breeds in Siberia and northern Japan visiting the Chinese coasts in winter.

White-winged Black Tern *Chlidonias leucopterus* 24cm

 In breeding plumage this is a beautiful tern with black head and underparts with grey wings, silvery tail and underwing. Rump and undertail coverts are white. Distinguished from Black Tern by less forked tail, black rather than white wing lining and short red rather than black bill. Legs orange red. Winter plumage is pale grey and white with dark grey crown patch and black line through ear coverts. Flight is even and straight with less swooping than Black Tern. Call a short *kek kek*, less raucous than most terns. Breeds in northeast China and winters in the lower Yangtze and southern coasts.

Rock Dove *Columba livia* 34cm

 Medium-sized pigeon with slaty-grey head. Plumage mostly grey, but mantle and side of neck have metallic green sheen and breast has purplish sheen. Wing has two characteristic black transverse bars, and tail has black terminal bar with outer feathers edged white. Some races have white rump. Call is soft muffled cooing *dru–oo–u*. Flies with rapid flappy flight, rising with clap of wings. This is a common bird of rocky cliffs as well as semi-deserts and farmland in west China and the Himalayas up to 4,000m. Feral populations occur in many parts of the country and on Hainan and Taiwan.

57

Adult (left); in flight (above)

Unmistakable pigeon. Head dark grey; collar, lower back and underparts white; upper back brownish-grey; rump black. Tail is black with broad white medial band. Wings are grey with two black bars. Eye is yellow and feet are red. This is a beautiful graceful pigeon that glides over the alpine pastures, rocky cliffs and snowfields at high altitudes in west and north-central China and Tibet. It lives in pairs or small flocks. It is absent from dry montane steppes but is quite common in suitable habitat, especially in the Himalayas.

Oriental Turtle Dove *Streptopelia orientalis* 32cm

Pinkish dove, distinguished from Spotted Dove by bold black and whitish striped patch on neck, rufous-edged dark-scalloped plumage on upperparts and grey rump. Tail is blackish with pale grey edge. Underparts generally pinkish. Feet are red. Distinguished from Eurasian Turtle Dove by larger size. The species lives in pairs and feeds mostly on the ground in open agricultural areas and around villages and monasteries. The call is a melodious *kroo kroo–kroo kroo*. This is a widespread and common species. Large flocks pass through southern China on spring passage. Occurs up to high altitudes in the Himalayas.

Red Turtle Dove *Streptopelia tranquebarica* 23cm

Small vinaceous-red dove with diagnostic white-bordered black collar at rear of neck. Male has greyish head, pinkish underparts and cinnamon wing-coverts. Blackish primaries and slaty tail with white edges and outer tips. Female is paler and duller, with dull brown head and less red in plumage. The call is a deep *cru–u–u–u–u*, repeated several times, with emphasis on first note. Feeds on the ground in busy searching walk. A common bird in south and east China in open woodlands and drier coastal forests. Regular winter visitor to Hong Kong.

Spotted Dove *Streptopelia chinensis* 30cm

Smallish pink dove with white-spotted black patch on rear side of neck. Crown is grey, rest of upperparts are generally brown and underparts are pink. Feet are red. Tail is blackish with white tips to outer feathers. The call is a melodious *ter–ku–koor*. Feeds on the ground and takes flight with a noisy clatter of wings. Often sits on roads or perches on telephone wires. Courtship display flight involves vertical climb followed by steep dive. This is a common and widespread, pair-living bird of open and agricultural areas, usually close to villages. These doves are sometimes caught as cage pets.

Emerald Dove *Chalcophaps indica* 25cm

Compact, small bronze-backed pigeon. Forehead and crown are white against the grey of the rest of head. Lower back dark grey, with two pale bands across rump. Tail is centrally black with barred outer feathers. Bill and feet red. Female and young are duller; young have barred underparts. The Emerald Dove lives mostly on the ground and inhabits some dense, dark parts of the forest. It flies at great speed close to the ground. The call is a long mournful note. It is a rather solitary bird, but not rare in southern China, south-east Tibet and Hainan.

Green Imperial Pigeon *Ducula aenea* 42cm

Large, robust arboreal pigeon with grey head and underparts, dark cinnamon vent and bronzy-green wings, back and tail. Distinguished from Mountain Imperial Pigeon by greener back and lack of broad tail bar. The call is a melodious, deep *click–hrooo*. They live in pairs or small flocks. They feed on figs, wild nutmegs and other fruit in the forest canopy and fly strongly between forests in search of food. The species is found throughout the tropical-forest zone of southern China at low altitudes, but is hunted for food and no longer common.

Derbyan Parakeet *Psittacula derbiana* 43cm

Large, long-tailed parrot with bright red upper bill, violet blue-grey head and breast and broad black moustachial stripe. Has greenish wash around eyes and forehead, and a narrow black frontal band extending into narrow eye-line. Tail is graduated, with bluish central feathers. Distinguished from other parakeets by grey breast and lack of maroon on 'shoulder' of wing. The call is a high-pitched shrill whistle. Flies fast over forest in screeching flocks. This is a common bird in hill and montane forests of central and south-west China at up to 4,000m. Commonly caught at nest for pet trade and locally endangered by such collecting.

Greater Coucal *Centropus sinensis* 49cm

Large black and chestnut cuckoo. Head, mantle, throat and breast glossy blue-black. Wings and middle of back rich chestnut. Tail is elongated and graduated, glossy green-black. Bill and feet shiny black, with bright red iris. Distinguished from Lesser Coucal by larger size and brighter, tidier plumage. Immature brown, banded and spotted with buff. The call is a deep *glug glug glug*. Keeps close to the ground. A common bird of scrub and grassland at the edge of forest and woodlands in southern China, unlike the more open-country Lesser Coucal.

Barn Owl *Tyto alba* 35cm

Unmistakable white owl with heart-shaped facial disc and black beady eyes. Underside almost pure white. Upperparts creamy-buff with delicate patterns of black and white on feather shafts. Feet are yellow. Lives in old buildings and hunts for small mammals in towns and over open ground. Hovers when hunting, and flight is silent owing to soft filaments on flight feathers. Call is a harsh screech. At rest assumes a contracted stick-like appearance, but when frightened performs a curious rocking display with head lowered and wings outstretched. Generally rare.

Collared Scops-owl *Otus lempiji* 23cm

Small brown owl with broad, prominent 'ear' tufts, bright buff nuchal collar and dark eyes. The eyebrows are buffy-white; underparts are mottled blackish. Immature is barred with dark brown. This is a nocturnal owl with a characteristic soft, hollow *hoo–o*, repeated several times per minute and with emphasis on the first note. The bird often calls from a prominent and low perch and can be readily located by torchlight. It is not so shy. This is a common bird over most of the country in forest, woodlands and gardens. It is regularly eaten as a medicinal soup in China.

Eurasian Eagle Owl *Bubo bubo* 69cm

Huge owl with long 'ear' tufts and enormous orange eyes. Colour is mottled and streaky brown. Breast is yellowish, boldly streaked dark brown, with each feather finely barred brown. Feathers extend on to toes. The call is a hollow *poop*. When found in daytime it is aggressively mobbed by crows and gulls. Alarmed birds assume a wide display posture with wings arched and head lowered. Gives beak-clicking sounds. Flies fast, with shallow wingbeats. Inhabits mountainous terrain with woods, generally nesting on cliffs (rarely on ground). Widespread but generally rare.

Snowy Owl *Nyctea scandiaca* 61cm

Unmistakable huge white owl with yellow eyes and generally spotted with black (feather tips) on crown, back, wings and lower breast, making the bird appear grey against snow. Partly diurnal but also active after dusk, hunting voles and picas. Sometimes sits on prominent rock or mound. Nests on the ground. Male gives duck-like alarm call, *krek–krek–krek*. Female has a barked alarm call and also gives whistled *'seeuee'* calls. Lives in open country at northern latitudes in both north-east and north-west China. Often migrates in winter. Generally rare.

Collared Owlet *Glaucidium brodiei* 16cm

Tiny brown owl without 'ear' tufts and with bright yellow eyes. Upperparts barred pale and rich brown. Underparts buff with bold streaks. Eyebrows are white, and there is a white collar around the front of the neck. At the back of neck is a bold black and white imitation face pattern which confuses small mobbing birds. The owlet calls repeatedly during the daytime with an easily imitated call, *poop poop–a–poop*. Sometimes active by day and flies with a fast buzzing flight. Feeds mostly on large insects. Generally rather common in suitable lowland and hill forests.

White-throated Kingfisher *Halcyon smyrnensis* 28cm

Brightly coloured kingfisher with turquoise back, wings and tail contrasting against rich chestnut-brown of head, upper mantle and belly. Throat and breast form white bib. Primaries are black, feet crimson and bill is scarlet. In flight, there is a conspicuous white wing patch at base of primaries. Call is a loud piercing cry, *kee–kee–kee–kee*. This is a common bird on ponds, along rivers, along coast and on flooded rice fields; it often perches on telephone wires. Nests in holes in banks. Found throughout south, east and central China and Hainan.

Common Kingfisher *Alcedo atthis* 18cm

Small, dazzling kingfisher. Upperparts shimmering, pale greenish-blue; underparts cinnamon-rufous with white chin and throat. There is a white spot on the side of the neck, and the orange ear-coverts distinguish this species from similar-sized Blue-eared Kingfisher and much larger Blyth's Kingfisher. Bill is black and feet red. The call is a shrill *peep peep*, often given in rapid flight. This is a common bird on small ponds, along streams, in mangroves and on flooded rice fieds; it often sits on telephone wires. Formerly persecuted for its feathers, used to make jewellery.

Blue-throated Bee-eater *Merops viridis* 28cm

Unmistakable bee-eater with deep chestnut crown and mantle, blue throat, back and tail, and green breast and wings. There is a black band through the eye. Central tail feathers are elongated in adults. Immature birds are like adult but duller, with crown and nape green. This is a bird of open woodlands, streams and gardens. Small flocks perch on bare branches and make gliding flights after insects. The call is a fast trilling *kerik–kerik–kerik*. The species breeds in east China and Hainan in holes in banks, but migrates south in winter through southern China and on to Indonesia.

Indian Roller *Coracias benghalensis* 33cm

Bluish-grey bird with slender decurved black bill. At rest looks dull, but at close range a beautiful mixture of turquoise-blue crown, tail-coverts and wings; lilac throat, upper mantle and part of flight feathers; and dull greenish back and central tail feathers. In flight, the brilliant blue in wings and tail is very conspicuous. The call is a harsh crow-like *chak chak*. Distinguished from Dollarbird by black bill, and from Blue Roller by less blue on head and breast. An occasional bird of open country and farmland in south and south-west China and southern Tibet.

Eurasian Hoopoe *Upupa epops* 28cm

Unmistakable boldly patterned bird with long, black-tipped crest. Head, base of crest and upper body cinnamon, lower back and all flight feathers boldly striped black and white. Eye, decurved bill and feet dark. Crest is erected when excited; otherwise carried flat, giving characteristic shape to head. Nests in holes in cliffs, buildings and trees. Feeds by probing with long bill in open ground, constantly changing direction. The call is a soft double or triple *hoo–poo–(poo)* and harsh shrieks. Widespread and generally quite common up to quite high altitudes.

Great Hornbill *Buceros bicornis* 125cm

 A huge pied hornbill with large yellow bill and flattened, concave casque. The eye is bright red in male and whitish in female. The white wing-bar and neck are often stained yellow. The white tail with broad subterminal black bar is diagnostic. Lives in pairs and nests in large tree holes. It feeds on fruits, especially figs. The call is a loud, far-carrying *wer–gok*, and the wingbeats are audible in flight. It occurs in the tropical areas of south-east Tibet and south-west China, but is now very rare in most of its former haunts as a result of hunting and habitat loss.

Great Barbet *Megalaima virens* 30cm

 Very large, big-headed barbet with dark inky-blue head and massive straw-coloured bill. Upperparts mostly green, belly yellow, streaked with dark green, and undertail-coverts bright red. Has heavy rising and falling flight like a woodpecker. The usual call is a constantly repeated cry like that of a cat, but the bird makes other calls including a loud rasp. These birds feed on soft fruits, including figs, and nest in tree holes. Resident and quite common in evergreen forests of southern China up to moderate altitudes of over 2,000m.

67

Blue-throated Barbet *Megalaima asiatica* 20cm

Green barbet with diagnostic crimson forecrown and hindcrown with black or bluish midcrown. Ocular region, face, throat and side of neck bright blue. There is a red spot on each side of breast. The call is a continuous fast repeated *took–a–rook*, *took–a–rook*, given by a bird sitting motionless in the treetops. Often found feeding in small parties in fig trees. A common bird of tropical evergreen forest and secondary forest at lower altitudes in south-east Tibet and south and south-west China. It is the commonest barbet in south-west Yunnan.

Great Spotted Woodpecker *Dendrocopos major* 24cm

The familiar Great Spotted Woodpecker is the most widespread woodpecker in China; found throughout temperate woodlands and farmlands. The boldly pied male has a narrow red nape band, lacking on the female. Both sexes have a red vent, but lack of red or orange on the black-streaked white breast distinguishes them from related Crimson-breasted and Rufous-bellied Woodpeckers. The Great Spotted is typical of the group, nesting in excavated tree holes and feeding on insects and grubs under tree bark. Birds drum loudly and have a loud, explosive call.

Long-tailed Broadbill *Psarisomus dalhousiae* 27cm

Beautiful green broadbill. Sexes alike. The long blue tail and the green plumage with a yellow, black and blue head pattern are quite distinctive. In flight, there is a whitish patch (bluish above at base of primaries). The species nests in a suspended ball-nest close to and often hanging over a stream. Has pleasant clear shrill whistled call notes. It feeds on insects, often catching prey in flight with an audible snap of the large bill. This species is quite common in the southern tropical and subtropical parts of the Himalayas and south China in evergreen broadleaf forests and open woodlands.

Hooded Pitta *Pitta sordida* 19cm

Adult has mostly black head with dark brown crown, green body, bright shining blue wing-coverts and rump and rosy-crimson lower belly and vent. Short tail is black, tipped with blue, and primaries are black with white panel, which shows as conspicuous patch in flight. Immature is duller, with more white on wing and pale brown throat and pinkish belly. Call is characteristic two-noted fluted whistle, *rew-rew*. Rests at night on low open perch. This is a rare bird, found hopping about on the forest floor in evergreen lowland and hill forests of south-east Tibet and south-west China.

69

Blue-winged Pitta *Pitta moluccensis* 21cm

Colourful pitta with contrasting buff eyebrow on otherwise black head, white throat, cinnamon-buff breast and rosy-crimson centre to belly. Back is green, with shining blue wing-coverts and rump. Short tail is black and primaries are black with white panel, which forms conspicuous patch in flight. Immature is duller and has no crimson on underparts. Voice is three-note whistle, *pu–wi–u*, with raised second note. This is a rare bird in lowland evergreen forests and scrub of south-east Tibet and south-west China.

Barn Swallow *Hirundo rustica* 15cm

Slim swallow with dark blue upperparts and white underparts. Forehead and throat are red and there is a dark blue gorget around throat. Tail is deeply forked, longer when breeding. Outspread tail has white band. Juvenile is duller, with less forked tail. Mud nests are made under eaves of houses or in recesses. Birds gather in flocks to migrate south in autumn. Rests on telephone wires and prominent perches. The flight is jerky and fast, interspersed with short glides after insects, often flying low over rivers and lakes. Call is a sharp *wit–wit*. Very common in towns and villages over the whole country.

White Wagtail *Motacilla alba* 19cm

Pied plumage with large white patch on wing-coverts and side of head. Upperparts variable with race and season; nape may be black, but mantle mostly grey. Underparts white, with varying extent of black on breast. Long tail black with white outer feathers. Immature ashy-grey with olive tinge above; white underparts mottled black on breast. Walks fast with constant tail-flicking. Call is hard *chissick*. A common bird throughout China in open areas, near water and in rice fields; often rests on roads. Several races show winter migrations southwards.

Grey–chinned Minivet *Pericrocotus solaris* 18cm

Male (above); female (right)

Smallish minivet with pale throat. Male is black and orangish-red with diagnostic grey chin, throat and cheeks. Female has yellow in place of red, whitish throat and grey crown, nape and mantle; separated from other female minivets by lack of yellow on forehead. Has partial whitish eye-ring. Juvenile has pale underparts but yellow or red wingbar. Voice is repeated thin *tsee see tsee*. Lives in large flocks that work noisily through upper and lower canopies of forest when feeding. Rather common and not shy in more open lowland forests in south-east Tibet, south and central China and Taiwan at up to 1,800m.

Crested Finchbill *Spizixos crinifrons* 22cm

Distinctive large olive–green bulbul with thick, ivory-coloured, finch–like bill and prominent crest. Underparts are greenish-yellow. Distinguished from Collared Finchbill by grey forehead and cheeks, lack of white throat collar and larger crest. Has broad black terminal band to tail. Birds live singly or in small flocks in open woodland, clearings, scrub and gardens at up to 3,000m. Sometimes perch on telephone wires. Calls with fluty cheerful phrases similar to those of other bulbuls. This is a common bird of open country, secondary forest and farmland throughout much of southern and central China.

Black–headed Bulbul *Pycnonotus atriceps* 17cm

Forest bulbul characterized by yellow plumage with black primaries, short-crested black head with bluish eyes and a yellow outer edge to the black rear tail. Distinguished from Black–crested Bulbul by lack of prominent crest, eye colour, black subterminal band to tail and yellow tip to tail. Less gregarious than other bulbuls, generally feeding alone in the middle storeys of the rainforest. The song is a soft, sweet simple phrase. A common tropical species found only in evergreen forests in the south-west of China at up to 1,800m.

Red–whiskered Bulbul *Pycnonotus jocosus* 20cm

Active brown bulbul with white underparts and red vent. Easily distinguished from the Red–vented Bulbul by its long pointed black crest and red and white patch over ear-coverts. The throat is white. The bird lives in noisy, lively groups which feed on small fruits and insects and keep up a lively chattering or give rather non-musical repetitive phrases of simple song, '*bulbi bulbit*'. The Red-whiskered Bulbul is a very common and familiar bird of gardens, secondary forest and scrub over extensive areas of southern China at up to 1,500m. It is one of the commonest birds in Hong Kong.

Light–vented Bulbul *Pycnonotus sinensis* 19cm

Small olive bulbul distinguished by a broad white stripe immediately behind the eye and extending right around the nape, slightly crested black crown, black moustache line and white vent. Juvenile has olive head and grey breast bar. Active flocks crowd fruit trees and give typical chattering chirps and simple-phrased, non–musical calls. Sometimes flycatches from perch. This is a common and familiar gregarious bird of forests, scrub, mangroves and gardens over central and southern China. One of the commonest birds in Hong Kong.

 Large, noisy bulbul with long, straggly crest of pointed feathers, olive upperparts, grey side of head, yellow underparts and white puffy-bearded throat. Distinguished with some difficulty from White–throated Bulbul by having duller underparts with paler yellow on belly. Lives in small parties that utter constant discordant cries and occasional weak song. It is aggressive in mobbing birds of prey. Active in lower layers of the forest, in mixed flocks. This is a very common bird in lowland evergreen and open forest of south-west China and Hainan.

Mountain Bulbul *Hypsipetes mcclellandii* 24cm

 Large, noisy olive-coloured bulbul with a spiky short crest, a rufous nape and upper breast and streaky whitish throat. Crown is dark brown with whitish streaking. Back, wings and tail are greenish, abdomen and vent whitish. Birds feed on small fruits and insects and sometimes form large flocks. The song is a sibilant monotonous three-note call, a rising three-note call and various mewing calls. Aggressively mobs raptors and cuckoos. This is a common flock- or pair-living bird of montane forests and scrub between 1,000 and 2,700m from the Himalayas to southern China.

Chestnut Bulbul *Hypsipetes castanonotus* 21cm

Large, smart bulbul with rich chestnut-brown upperparts and slightly crested black crown, white throat and whitish abdomen. Breast and flanks pale grey. Wings and tail greyish-brown. The white throat is sometimes puffed out like that of the Criniger Bulbul, but the species is distinctive. It lives in small active parties and has loud scolding notes and sharp ringing call, *tickety boo*. Keeps to rather dense thickets. A familiar species of the lowland forests of southern China and becoming more common in Hong Kong as forests grow more mature.

Black Bulbul *Hypsipetes leucocephalus* 20cm

White-headed form (above)

Black bulbul with slightly forked tail and bright red bill, feet and eye. Some have white head, and western races have greyish foreparts. Distinguished from Silky Starling by darker breast and back. Immature is greyish. Has slight flattish crest. Calls variable, including loud squawks, twitters and strident whistles. A common call is a nasal cat–like mewing. Feeds on fruits and insects. A common bird of evergreen hill forests in Himalayas and south and central China, Hainan and Taiwan, and shows some seasonal movements. In winter months, large flocks of several hundred birds can be found in southern China.

Blue–winged Leafbird *Chloropsis cochinchinensis* 18cm

Active green canopy–living bird with blue wing edges. Male has black lores and throat with purplish-blue moustachial streaks. Black bib is edged yellow. Yellowish tinge to head. Distinguished from Orange–bellied Leafbird by yellowish–green breast. Lacks golden forehead of Golden–fronted Leafbird. Female has blue on throat and wings, but otherwise almost entirely green. It makes many loud lively calls, often imitating other species. Particularly fond of flowering *Erythrina* trees. A common bird in lowland evergreen forests of south-west China.

Golden–fronted Leafbird *Chloropsis aurifrons* 19cm

Bright green leafbird of forest canopy. Adult has purplish-blue throat surrounded by black bib fringed yellow, and has shining blue shoulder patch. Forehead is golden. Immature is all green, with bluish malar stripe and shoulder patch. Lacks distinctive orange belly of next species. The call is a loud cheerful *che–wit, che–wit* and a melodious song, but the bird is also a good mimic of many other bird calls. This is an active bird of the high canopy, visiting flowering trees, especially *Erythrina* and *Bombax*. Occurs in tropical deciduous forests of south-east Tibet and south-west China at up to 2,300m.

Orange–bellied Leafbird *Chloropsis hardwickii* 20cm

This is the commonest leafbird in the country, found throughout the hills and montane forests of southern China and Hainan. The male is very colourful, characterized by green upperparts and rich orange underparts, with blue wings and tail and a black mask and bib with blue moustachial streak. The female is mostly green with bluish moustachial streak and only a narrow ochre band in the centre of the abdomen. It is an active insectivore of all canopy layers and has a loud, clear song and whistled call notes, often mimicking other birds' calls.

Asian Fairy–bluebird *Irena puella* 28cm

The male is an elegant mixture of black with contrasting and dazzling blue on the crown extending over the entire back, vent and tail-coverts. The eye is bright red. The female is all over greenish-blue. The species is predominantly frugivorous and is

Male (left); Female (right)

a common visitor to fruiting fig trees. The call is a loud, clear and distinctive *pip*, often given in flight, and a sharp *be quick, be quick, be quick*, or loud mellow song. This is a common and noisy bird of the high canopy in evergreen forests of south-west China at up to 1,400m. Sometimes forms large flocks.

77

Maroon-backed Accentor *Prunella immaculata* 15cm

Small, shy accentor with pale yellow eyes, generally grey plumage, but chestnut brown back, tertials and cinnamon vent. Grey crown feathers scaled with whitish tips; primary coverts black, primaries black with whitish edges. Sexes alike. A forest bird found in undergrowth of dense mossy conifer forests and scrub between 2800m and 4200m along eastern Himalayas, north Yunnan, west Sichuan and extreme south of Gansu province. In winter they are found in secondary scrub and forest edge down to about 1500m. Call is a monotonous, *zee dzit*.

Alpine Accentor *Prunella collaris* 17cm

Head and central underparts ashy-brown, flanks rich chestnut, undertail-coverts black with white edging, and throat white, spotted with black. Wing-coverts black, with white tips and bars. Primaries are brown with rufous edges. Tail is blackish with a white tip. Bill yellow at base. Generally single or in pairs. Often sits on prominent rock. Common in scrub and bare areas of alpine meadows above treeline through north-east and north-central China, Himalayas and Tibetan plateau. Populations that breed in the north-east winter in eastern provinces.

White-browed Shortwing *Brachypteryx montana* 13cm

Male is slaty-blue with partly concealed short white brow and lores. Female is brown with whitish belly and white brow. Wings and tail are short, and the birds stay close to the ground in dense cover and bamboo patches of montane forests. This species lives at generally higher altitudes than the Brown Shortwing and is distinguished by longer tail and dark underparts of male. Has loud sweet song. This species is found in central China and Tibet and on mountains of southern China.

Japanese Robin *Erithacus akahige* 15cm

Similar to European Robin, with brown upperparts, orange face and breast and greyish flanks. Male has narrow black gorget surrounding orange bib. Distinguished from male Red-breasted Flycatcher by lack of white patches at base of tail. Female similar but duller. Immature is scaly and brown. Cocks tail repeatedly. The call is a distinctive sweet trill. The species breeds in Japan but migrates in winter to southern China, where it is a scarce bird of forest and woodlands.

Rufous-tailed Robin *Luscinia sibilans* 13cm

The Rufous-tailed Robin is a graceful but rather nondescript robin. The upperparts are olive-brown with a rufous tail, and the underparts are whitish, scalloped with olive on the breast. Distinguished from other female robins and flycatchers by rufous tail. Has a short sweet song. This is a rather terrestrial robin, keeping to floor or low vegetation in dense shady patches of forest and shivering its tail energetically. The species breeds in Siberia, but migrates through most of eastern China in winter.

Siberian Rubythroat *Luscinia calliope* 15cm

A beautiful bird with brown upperparts, a white supercilium and malar stripe and, on the male, a bold orange-scarlet throat patch outlined with a narrow black border (white on female). The underparts are buff, with a white centre to the belly. Distinguished from White-tailed Ruby-throat by narrower black border to throat bib and lack of white tail patches. Feeds on the ground in fairly open places, flicking its tail characteristically. It breeds in the north-east and centre of China and Tibet, but migrates to southern and eastern China in winter.

Siberian Blue Robin *Luscinia cyane* 15cm

 An elegant robin with slaty-blue upperparts and white underparts. The throat and breast are contrastingly edged black. Distinguished from similar Slaty-blue Flycatcher by entirely dark tail and lack of dark patches on side of breast, also by more terrestrial habits. Female brown with blue tail. Distinguished from female Red-flanked Bluetail by brown rather than rufous flanks. Largely terrestrial, staying in shady places beneath dense vegetation. It shivers its tail characteristically. Breeds in northeast China, but winters over most of the country.

Golden Bush Robin *Tarsiger chrysaeus* 15cm

 This is another elegant little robin. The male is rufous golden with a black mask, yellow eyebrow and olive crown, back and wings. Tail is yellow with black terminal bar and central feathers. Female is duller and more greenish with brown instead of black, to mask and tail. Immature like female, but streaky and scaled with black feather tips. Found in conifer forests, scrub and farmland, where it lives quietly among the lower storeys feeding mostly on insects. It breeds over much of northern China and in Tibet, but winters through the south of the country.

Blue-fronted Redstart *Phoenicurus frontalis* 16cm

Male has dark blue head, breast and upperparts with bright blue forehead and short eyebrow. Rump and belly rufous. Female rufous-brown, distinguished from Daurian Redstart by lack of white wing patch. Both sexes distinguished by tail pattern, with dark central feathers and dark tips to outer rufous feathers giving dark 'T' pattern on spread tail. Grating alarm call and simple *tchih tchih*, given from prominent low perch. A common bird of scrubby and rocky mountains and highlands throughout central China and Tibet. Migrates south in winter.

River Chat *Chaimarrornis leucocephalus* 19cm

Unmistakable black and chestnut bird with white crown and nape. The rump, base of tail and belly are chestnut. Immature is duller and brownish, with crown scaled black. A very common bird along mountain streams and rivers over most of China and in the Himalayas, habitually sitting on prominent rocks in or close to water, bobbing head on alighting and flicking tail continuously. Courtship involves curious head-weaving display. Breeds in headwaters up to high altitudes of over 4,000m, moving downriver in winter. Call a shrill, rather plaintive *t–e–e–e–*.

White-tailed Robin *Cinclidium leucurum* 17cm

Male is a very dark blue robin, with white flashes in base of tail and cobalt-blue forecrown. Throat and breast are black, with usually concealed white spot on side of neck and on breast. Female is brown, with whitish transverse band on base of throat; tail as male. Immature is like female but with rufous streaks. Has a powerful sweet song. A shy bird of very dark thickets in evergreen forests. Breeds in montane forests above 1,000m in south-east Tibet and central and southern China, but migrates to lowlands in winter.

Oriental Magpie-robin *Copsychus saularis* 23cm

A common black and white songster of southern China. The male has a black head, throat and back. The wings are black with a conspicuous forked white wingbar, and the white tail is centrally black. The underparts are white. The female is similar, but mostly charcoal-grey in place of black. The birds are cocky and sit on exposed perches flicking their longish tail, drooping their wings and singing with a clear melodious voice. The alarm call is a harsh clicking. It lives in open forest, secondary scrub and gardens. Feeds mostly on the ground.

White-rumped Shama *Copsychus malabaricus* 28cm

The White-rumped Shama is one of the most melodious birds in China. It is similar to the related magpie-robin, but has much longer black central tail feathers and has a chestnut belly and vent. The shama is more of a forest bird and keeps to rather shady and dense parts of the forest undergrowth. The alarm call is a harsh click similar to the magpie-robin's, but the song is much richer and more melodious. The species feeds mostly on the ground and is confined to tropical areas of the extreme south of China, where it is not so common. This is a favourite species for the cagebird trade because of its excellent song.

Blue Whistling-thrush *Myiophoneus caeruleus* 33cm

Large inky-blue thrush which looks black in poor light. In good light, diagnostic blue spangles glint on head, back and breast. Juvenile is duller, without spangles. Some races have yellow bill; otherwise black, as feet. Call is a penetrating harsh whistle, or a screech of alarm similar to that of forktail. This is a common skulker of montane-forest undergrowth or rocky bluffs and scrub near streams. It often comes out into open clearings and sometimes perches on a prominent rock, flicking tail. Lives in Himalayas, and mountains of central, eastern and southern China.

Plain-backed Mountain Thrush *Zoothera mollissima* 26cm

Medium-sized, boldly marked, shy thrush with reddish brown uniform upperparts, scaly belly and black-streaked throat showing conspicuous white patch. Dense scaling on upper throat almost forms black gorget. Obvious white eye-ring. Lack of barring on back distinguishes from Scaly Thrush and lack of pale eyebrow distinguishes from Mistle Thrush. Virtual lack of white wing bars at rest distinguishes from Long-tailed Mountain Thrush. Locally common in dense forests and treeline scrub from 2400m and 4200m in the Himalayas, southeast Tibet, north Yunnan and west Sichuan. Winters at lower altitudes. Rattling alarm call like Common Blackbird.

Scaly Thrush *Zoothera dauma* 30cm

Strikingly large, scaly thrush. Underparts broadly scaled by bold black crescents. Upperparts uniquely scaled with black-edged feathers of crown, nape and mantle. Tertials boldly tipped white. Outer black tail feathers tipped white. Throat and side of head also scaly, but ear-coverts paler and bounded by blackish margin. In flight, the two conspicuous white bars are visible on otherwise blackish underwing. Flight is fast and undulating. A shy forest bird which flies up to freeze high in canopy when disturbed. Breeds in north-east China and Himalayas, but winters in forest and woodlands of south China.

85

Siberian Thrush *Zoothera sibirica* 24cm

Male is distinct, with slaty-blue plumage, bold white eyebrow and white abdomen. Female is brown with rufous wings, scaly barring on breast and flanks and complex patterning on side of face, with white eyebrow curling downwards around streaked ear-coverts. In flight, displays two conspicuous white bars on underwing typical of *Zoothera* species. Sits very upright in branches and is quite approachable. Breeds in open grassy hills over much of north-east China, but winters in southern woodlands.

Orange-headed Thrush *Zoothera citrina* 22cm

Unmistakable thrush with grey back, orange head and breast and white abdomen and vent. There is a white wingbar, and most individuals have one or two blackish bars on side of head. Legs are yellow. Female and juvenile have olive-brown back. This is a ground-living thrush favouring shady quiet places in woodlands, forest and gardens. It is rather shy. Call, often uttered in flight, is buzzing *dzee dzee*. Widespread but never common over much of southern China.

Common Blackbird *Turdus merula* 28cm

Male black with orange-yellow bill, slight eye-ring and black feet. Female blackish-brown above, dark brown below, and has a dark greenish-yellow to black bill. Distinguished from Grey-winged Blackbird by uniformly dark wing. Sweet song is less musical than that of European races, but rattling alarm call is much the same. The blackbird feeds on the ground, in search of invertebrates, probing for worms and, in winter, eating fruits and berries. It is a common bird of woodlands, parks and gardens over most of China at up to 4,000m.

Black-breasted Thrush *Turdus dissimilis* 23cm

Male has entirely black head, mantle and breast. The back is dark grey and wings and tail are black. Lower breast and flanks are diagnostically bright chestnut and central belly and vent are white. Female is dark olive above, with white chin and throat streaked black and white. Breast is olive-grey, spotted with black. Vent is white. Wings blackish and tail dark olive. Feeds mostly on the ground. This is a fairly common though shy and solitary thrush of mountains and hills in southern China in scrub, forest and woodlands.

Eyebrowed Thrush *Turdus obscurus* 24cm

Elegant brown thrush with grey head and bright cinnamon-orange breast band and flanks. Both sexes have white eyebrow and white line below eye. Female has whitish streaky throat. Immature has pale wingbar. A shy forest thrush, keeping to dense thickets and only rarely venturing to feed in open areas. Lives in small flocks which fly up to freeze in treetops when disturbed. Call is thin *tzee*. Breeds in northern Asia, but migrates south to winter in woodlands over much of southern China. Generally scarce, but some large wintering flocks encountered.

White-crowned Forktail *Enicurus leschenaulti* 28cm

Large forktail with long, deeply forked black and white graduated tail, white crown and entirely black mantle and black breast. Distinguished from Slaty-backed Forktail by black mantle and from Spotted Forktail by lack of white spots on back. Lives along rocky rivers and streams in forest, perching on rocks with flicking tail and shyly flying off with loud cries when observed. Alarm call is harsh screech like that of Blue Whistling-thrush. Slightly more montane than Slaty-backed, but often found on the same rivers together. This is a common bird in suitable narrow habitat in central and south-west China.

Pale-footed Bush-warbler *Cettia pallidipes* 12cm

Small olive-brown warbler with buff eyebrow and white underparts. Flanks and vent buffish. Characterized by fleshy pale feet and nearly square tail. Difficult to identify in the field, but distinguished from Dusky Warbler by lack of rufous tinge on eyebrow and flanks. Distinguished from Stub-tailed Bush-warbler by longer tail and lack of dark edges on crown feathers. A shy skulker in the undergrowth of forest and secondary scrub, often feeding on ground. Voice is a series of sharp chirps. Common in lowlands of south-west China up to 1,500m.

Common Tailorbird *Orthotomus sutorius* 12cm

Tiny olive bird with rufous crown and long cocked tail. Underparts whitish, with buff flanks. Tail of male longer than that of female. Immature lacks rufous on head. Distinguished from Black-throated Tailorbird by white vent, duller underparts, longer tail and lack of black on throat, but dusky feather bases on throat can give impression of dark patches. Keeps on the move in dense undergrowth or occasionally climbs into canopy to sing. Varied calls include noisy repeated *ch–wee ch–wee ch–wee* and monotonous wren-like song. This is a common bird of secondary scrub, bamboo and gardens in south China.

Golden-spectacled Warbler *Seicercus burkii* 13cm

Yellowish warbler with broad greenish-grey coronal stripe bordered on each side by black browline and with yellow underparts. Inner web of outer tail feathers white. Yellow eye-ring separates it from White-spectacled and Greycheeked Warblers. Some races have single yellow wingbar. Call is loud *chip chiwoo*. Breeds in montane forest and woodlands at 1,800–3,600m, keeping mostly to lower storeys. Found in Himalayas, Tibet and mountains of central and south-east China. Migrates south in winter and visits lowlands. Regular visitor to Hongkong.

White-tailed Leaf Warbler *Phylloscopus davisoni* 10cm

Smallish green leaf warbler with yellowish underparts distinguished from most similar warblers by orange-yellow lower mandible, broad pale crown stripe and prominent wing bars. Difficult to distinguish in field from Blyth's Leaf Warbler but in hand can be seen to have outer two tail feathers mostly white rather than only bordered white. Song is a sweet shrill warble. Breeding and resident in southern China and only partly migratory. A common bird of deciduous and mixed woodlands and hill forests.

Buff-barred Warbler *Phylloscopus pulcher* 12cm

Small leaf warbler with brownish-olive back and faint pale crown-stripe. Diagnostic rufous-buff wingbars. White inner web of outer tail feathers. Rump is pale yellow and underparts dirty yellow. Eyebrow not pronounced. Lower mandible is brownish-yellow with black tip. Lively warbler of forest canopy, sometimes joining mixed flocks. The call is a fine *zip* followed by a fast shrill trill. Breeds in north of range and in high mountains, but winters south and at lower altitudes. This is the commonest bird in conifer and rhododendron forests in Himalayas, Tibetan plateau and central China from 2,000 to 4,000m.

Grey-headed Flycatcher *Culicicapa ceylonensis* 13cm

Small flycatcher with diagnostic coloration of grey crested head and breast, bright greenish upperparts and bright yellow belly and vent. Distinguished from similar-coloured warblers by lack of head markings and by upright posture and behaviour. Makes regular fluttery, dashing flights after insects, returning to the same perch. Noisy, with regular chatter of sweet whistled *silly billy* and sharp, clear trilling and twittering. A common bird of lowland and hill forests of the Himalayas, south-east Tibet, central and south China.

91

Male is a large dark blue flycatcher. Underparts blackish, upperparts blue, with shiny cobalt crown, patch at side of neck, shoulder of wing and rump. Female is rufous-brown with rufous forehead and tail, grey nape and shiny blue patch on side of neck. Distinguished from similar-coloured Small Niltava by much larger size, lack of gorget and dark vent. Immature is brown with buff spots, and with blackish scaling on breast. Call is a clear whistle of three or four notes. This is an occasional bird of dense evergreen forests in south-east Tibet and south-west China at 1,000–2,500m. Shy and keeps to dark thickets.

Small Niltava *Niltava macgrigoriae* 14cm

Male is a very dark blue flycatcher with black side of face and throat and white vent. Forecrown, side of neck and rump are shining blue. Distinguished from Large Niltava by blue breast and white vent. Also by small size, brown nape and pale gorget. Female is brown with rufous wings and tail, shiny blue patch on side of neck, buff throat and pale buff gorget. Call is thin, high-pitched *twee–twee–ee–twee*, with second note highest. Fairly common in dense undergrowth of evergreen forest at 900–2,400m in south-east Tibet and south China.

Fujian Niltava *Niltava davidi* 18cm

Male is deep blue above and rufous below. Side of face is black, and forehead, small patch on neck, shoulder of wing and rump are bright iridescent blue. Distinguished with difficulty from Rufousbellied Niltava by darker colours. Female is greyishbrown with rufous-brown tail and wings. She has a white gorget on throat and small iridescent blue patch on side of neck. Distinguished from Rufousbellied by whiter belly.

Male (above); female (below)

This is a common flycatcher of dense forest undergrowth from the Himalayas to west and south China. Breeds in montane forests, but winters in lowlands. Occasional birds winter in Hong Kong.

White-tailed Flycatcher *Cyornis concretus* 15cm

Male (left);
female (above)

Male is dull blue, with black lores and white belly and vent. Forecrown is brighter blue. Central and outer tail feathers black, others white and distinctive in spread tail. Distinguished from White-tailed Robin by paler coloration and white belly. Female is brown, with white flashes in tail, white vent and sometimes concealed white gorget. Immature is brown, with rusty speckles above and dark scaling below. Song is loud three-note whistle, *where are you*, with second note highest. Keeps to dark undergrowth in evergreen forest at moderate altitude in south-east Tibet and south-west China.

Blue-and-white Flycatcher *Cyanoptila cyanomelana* 18cm

Male is a large black and white flycatcher. Side of face, throat and upper breast black. Upperparts otherwise blue at rest; abdomen, vent and patches at base of tail white. Race *cumatilis* is less bright, and black parts are deep greenish-blue. Female is rufescent olive-brown above, with dark primaries; chin and belly white, with greyish-brown flanks and white eye-ring. Breeds in north-east China, but winters in south-east and south China and Hainan. An occasional bird of mixed and deciduous forests, woodlands and gardens, often close to small streams.

Verditer Flycatcher *Eumyias thalassina* 17cm

Male is entirely greenish-blue with black lores. Female duller, with lores and chin whitish, speckled with grey. Immature is grey-brown with slight greenish tinge above, and grey below textured with scaly buff. Call is a loud sweet warble. Sits upright on prominent perch to hawk after flying insects. A fairly common bird in central and south China, with some seasonal movements. Sometimes very common when flocks are moving through a locality. Found in all forest types from 1,000 to 3,000m. Comes into plains in winter.

94

Asian Brown Flycatcher *Muscicapa dauurica* 13cm

Upright brownish-grey flycatcher with whitish eye-ring. Underparts are white, with grey wash across breast and on flanks. Wings are blackish with faint white bar, especially in autumn. Distinguished from Grey-streaked Flycatcher by lack of dark streaking on breast, and from Brown-breasted Flycatcher by lack of rufous edges on wings and lack of rufous tail. Call is a soft chatter. Sits quietly on prominent perch beneath main canopy generally solitary. Common and widespread, breeding in north-east, east and central China in open and mixed forests but migrating through south China to winter in south-east Asia.

Slaty Blue Flycatcher *Ficedula tricolor* 13cm

Male is small, dull bluish flycatcher with slaty blue upperparts, black sides of face and pale blue forehead. Tail is black with bold white basal flashes. Underparts are pinkish buff in western races and whitish in eastern races with brownish grey flanks and on breast. Female is dull brown with dark central tail feathers. Distinguished from similar Snowy-browed Flycatcher by lack of pale eyebrow. Common in mixed conifer forests between 1600m and 3000m in Himalayas, south-east Tibet, north Yunnan and central China. Winters south to Indochina.

Rufous-gorgeted Flycatcher *Ficedula strophiata* 14cm

Small, pretty forest-living flycatcher with white flashes at base of black tail. Upperparts mostly uniform greyish-brown; wings olive; underparts grey. Adult male has narrow white forehead and small scarlet gorget (often inconspicuous). Female is similar to male, but gorget is smaller and paler. Immature is streaky brown, with black scaling on rufous flanks. The usual call is a high-pitched, repeated *pink*; also gives low churring. This is a bird of the ground and lower bushes in closed forest in Tibet, and central and south China between 1,000 and 3,000m. It is rather common but quite shy.

Yellow-rumped Flycatcher *Ficedula zanthopygia* 13cm

Male is black and yellow with white wing patch. Distinguished from Narcissus Flycatcher by bold white rather than yellow eyebrow. Female is olive on crown, nape and mantle, with yellow rump and flanks; lacks white eyebrow. Distinguished from female Narcissus by less bold white wing patch and lack of yellow lores. A shy bird, keeping to dense undergrowth in forest, woodlands and gardens in hilly areas, usually close to streams. Breeds in north-east, east and central China, migrating through southern areas in winter. Generally rather uncommon.

Streak-breasted Scimitar-babbler *Pomatorhinus ruficollis*
22cm

Small rich brown scimitar-babbler with comparatively short yellow bill, bold long white eyebrow, rufous collar, white throat and rufous or olive underparts. The white throat and breast are heavily streaked olive-brown or chestnut. Culmen of bill blackish. Call is a loud three-noted hoot, with last note lowest. A common bird of hill forests and bamboo thickets, feeding on or near the ground. Found in hills of southern, central and eastern China, from Himalayas and south-east Tibet to Sichuan and Zhejiang, Taiwan and Hainan.

Spot-breasted Scimitar-Babbler *Pomatorhinus erythrocnemis*
27cm

Large scimitar-babbler without pale eyebrow and heavily spotted black on breast. Bill is dull, upperparts rich brown, and underparts grey or whitish with bright rufous side of head. Some races have rufous flanks and undertail-coverts. There is usually a black moustachial stripe. Several races vary in details. A common bird of dense scrub and open undergrowth and even grassland in south China and Taiwan. It is a shy bird and difficult to see, but has a loud, three-noted call with the last note being the highest.

Eyebrowed Wren-babbler *Napothera epilepidota* 10cm

Male (above)
Juvenile (below)

Tiny babbler with very short tail and distinctive prominent buffy-white eyebrow. Upperparts are brown with black scaling and white shaft streaks. Underparts are buffy-white, streaked brown, with rufous flanks. Wing-coverts tipped buffy-white. Immature lacks eyebrow and is spotted and fluffy. Mostly feeds on the ground, where it hops about like other wren-babblers. Calls include loud treble chatter, chuckling call and occasional sharp notes. This is a common bird in hill-forest undergrowth or secondary scrub in southern China and Hainan.

Golden Babbler *Stachyris chrysaea* 12cm

Unmistakable small active babbler with bright yellow underparts, dull yellow-olive upperparts, yellow streaks on crown and black lores. Distinguished from warblers by more triangular bill, black lores and voice. The song is a low-pitched whistle, *sweep–sweep–sweep–sweep*, with emphasis on first note; also rising sibilant call, *tzu–tzu–tzu*, and excited chattering. Often mixes with fulvettas and other species in 'bird waves'. Easily excited, and attracted by 'pishing'. This is a common bird in forest undergrowth in montane broadleaf and mixed forests of Himalayas, south Tibet and south-west China.

Grey-throated Babbler *Stachyris nigriceps* 13cm

Small brown babbler with streaked crown, whitish malar patch, black chin and throat and rusty-buff underparts. Distinguished from Spot-necked Babbler by cinnamon side of face and lack of white spots, black throat and dull underparts. Voice is a churring and clear *prrreee–prrreee* call. This is a common but skulking bird of forest undergrowth in the Himalayas, south-east Tibet and southern China. Easily attracted by 'pishing'. Prefers dense thickets close to small streams.

Spot-necked Babbler *Stachyris striolata* 16cm

Smallish brown babbler with white eyebrow, black side of face, white throat and diagnostic white spots on side of face. Upperparts are rich brown and underparts are bright rufous-chestnut. Upper breast has a few white streaks. Distinguished from Grey-throated Babbler by black side of face, white throat, white spots and richer rufous underparts. Call is a loud clear note. A common skulker in dense undergrowth, bamboo thickets and secondary growth, usually close to streams, in southern China and Hainan lowland evergreen-forest zone.

99

Striped Tit-babbler *Macronous gularis* 13cm

 Small flock-living babbler with rufous crown and yellow lores and eyebrow. Upperparts otherwise olive, and underparts are dull yellow with narrow black streaks on breast. Distinguished from Rufous-capped Babbler by less rufous cap, more yellow on abdomen and white iris. The calls include chittering, churring, and a resonant series of *choonk* notes at about three per second. This is a very common bird in secondary scrub and in dense tangles of vines and bushes along the side of streams and rivers in lowland evergreen forests of south-west China.

Bearded Tit *Panurus biarmicus* 17cm

 Slender cinnamon parrotbill with grey head, fine bill and, on male, diagnostic vertical tapering black moustachial stripe. Body is cinnamon-buff, with very long tail and black and white pattern on wings. Female lacks black on head, but juvenile male has black lores. Call is a twanging lively *pching* or twittering song. Lives in active flocks, clambering and hopping about in reedbeds and flying with weak rapid wingbeats, flocks sometimes working high into sky before diving back into reeds. Locally common in suitable reedy habitats in northern China.

Spot-breasted Parrotbill *Paradoxornis guttaticollis* 19cm

Distinctive large parrotbill with diagnostic black spots on breast. Bushy-crested crown and nape are orange-rufous and there is a conspicuous black patch over ear-coverts. Upperparts otherwise dull reddish-brown and underparts buffy. Bill is massive and orange-yellow and feet are bluish-grey. Voice is a rapid loud mellow whistle of eight to ten notes on the same pitch, also group chittering. Quite common in grassy scrub, secondary brush and reeds at moderate to high altitudes in south-east Tibet and central and southern China.

Vinous-throated Parrotbill *Paradoxornis webbianus* 12cm

Tiny pinkish-brown parrotbill with small yellow bill. Crown and wings are slightly rufous. Slight streaking on throat. Iris is brown and eye-ring not conspicuous. Wings edged rufous in some races. Distinguished from similar-sized Brown-winged and Ashy-throated Parrotbills by pinkish coloration. Lives in active flocks, generally in undergrowth and low bushes. Call is tiny continuous twittering. Easily attracted to soft 'pishing' calls. A common bird in scrub, thickets and forest edge at moderate altitudes in central, east and south-east China and Taiwan.

101

Golden Parrotbill *Paradoxornis verreauxi* 10cm

Pretty little parrotbill with orange crown, grey cheeks and whitish underparts. Has diagnostic black throat and upper breast with broad black eyebrow. Malar area is white, flanks are cinnamon. Back is yellowish brown and tail is brown but wings are black with white edges and conspicuous rufous panel. Distinguished from Black-throated and Black-browed Tits by thick bill. Call is plaintive bleats and churring notes. Lives in small flocks in undergrowth of broadleaf montane forests above 1,000m in southeast and southern China and Taiwan. Probably conspecific with Black-throated Parrotbill.

Chinese Babax *Babax lanceolatus* 28cm

Looks like a heavily streaked greyish-brown laughingthrush with narrowly barred tail, rather long scimitar bill and characteristic black moustachial stripe. Short crest can be partially erect. Iris is yellow. Call is a loud creaky wailing *ou–phee–ou–phee*, repeated several times. Lives in small groups and feeds mostly on the ground. Rather skulking in habits, but perches in prominent place to call. This is a common and noisy bird of scrub, thickets and undergrowth of open montane forests and hill forests in southern Tibet and central and southern China.

Masked Laughingthrush *Garrulax perspicillatus* 30cm

Greyish-brown laughingthrush with distinctive black forehead and mask. Has a slight crest. Upperparts brown, with black edge to tail. Underparts greyish on breast, grading to whitish abdomen with cinnamon vent. Lives in small groups that feed mostly on the ground. Flight is fast with long glides. Groups maintain chattering calls, but also have various laughing calls and loud piercing contact note, *piew piew piew*. This is a common and noisy lowland bird over most of east, south and central China in woods, gardens, bamboo thickets, parks and scrub. Generally not shy.

White-throated Laughingthrush *Garrulax albogularis* 28cm

Brown laughingthrush with diagnostic broad white throat patch, olive-brown breast bar and blue eyes. Forehead is rufous, grading to olive-brown on the crown; lores and below the eye are black. Abdomen is centrally white, with cinnamon flanks and vent. Tail is olive, with broad white tips to outer four pairs of feathers. Calls include group mutterings and harsh chorus. A common bird living in large noisy groups in montane conifer forests between 2,700 and 4,500m in central China, Tibet and Himalayas. A second, rufous-crowned race lives in the mountains of Taiwan.

White-crested Laughingthrush *Garrulax leucolophus* 30cm

Unmistakable laughingthrush with white-crested head crossed by black lower forehead, lores and eye-stripe. Several races vary in details, but upperparts are generally brown with varying grey on nape, whilst underparts are white with varying amounts of orange-brown on breast, belly and flanks. Lives in noisy groups which give loud maniacal cackling chorus, as well as various clear whistles and chatters. Birds feed mostly on the ground, noisily turning over leaves in search of insects. This is a common bird of dense thickets in secondary forests at up to 1,500m in the Himalayas and south-west China.

Greater Necklaced Laughingthrush *Garrulax pectoralis* 30cm

Rufous-brown laughingthrush with complex black and white patterning on head and breast. Distinguished from Lesser Necklaced Laughingthrush by black moustachial stripe separating pale breast from white-streaked ear-coverts. Flanks are rich rufous. Rufous tail is edged white or buff in flight. Flies with long glides. Calls include squeaky contact notes, bursts of group laughter and short whistles. This is a common group-living bird of hill forests at up to 1,500m in the Himalayas, south-west, central and east China, including Hainan.

Black-throated Laughingthrush *Garrulax chinensis* 23cm

Dark greyish laughingthrush with black face and throat, distinguished from Masked Laughingthrush by having white ear coverts and white edges to black, slightly bushy brow. Upperparts are uniform olive grey. Underparts olive grey becoming rufous ventrally. Wings have pale edged remiges and tail is tipped black. It has a cackling group alarm call and lives in small groups, feeding mostly on the ground or in undergrowth. A common bird of dense scrub, lowland forests and bamboo thickets in southern China. It is a favoured song bird and commonly seen for sale in bird markets.

Yellow-throated Laughingthrush *Garrulax galbanus* 23cm

Smallish pretty laughingthrush with bluish-grey crown, black mask and yellowish throat. Upperparts mostly brown and underparts buff with white vent. Tail has black terminal band tipped with white. Narrow white browline and white vent distinguish it from Yellow-breasted Laughingthrush. Calls less strident than most other laughingthrushes and include feeble chirps. Keeps to dense scrub, feeding among the floor litter like other laughingthrushes. A very rare pale race is known from south Yunnan but the species is slightly more common in the mountains of south-east China.

Barred Laughingthrush *Garrulax lunulatus* 23cm

 Smallish sandy-brown laughingthrush boldly scaled with black and buff crescents over back and flanks and with conspicuous whitish patch around eye. Tail is bluish-grey with black sub-terminal band and white tips. Edges of primaries are bluish. Feeds on the ground, busily scraping through leaf litter. Lives in small parties in the bamboo understorey of broadleaf and conifer forests through much of central China at moderate altitudes between 1,500 and 3,600m, where it is not uncommon.

Spotted Laughingthrush *Garrulax ocellatus* 31cm

 Large laughingthrush with black crown, nape and throat; boldly spotted upperparts and sides of breast. Lores, below eye and chin are pale buff. Upperparts brown, each feather marked with black crescentic spot with white tip. South Tibetan race has chestnut ear-coverts. Distinguished from Giant Laughingthrush by shorter tail and black throat. Occurs in small parties, keeping to undergrowth and feeding on ground. Call is a clear whistled song and harsh grating chorus. Several races occur between the Himalayas and central China in montane areas between 2,000 and 3,500m in forest. Not uncommon.

Rusty Laughingthrush *Garrulax poecilorhynchus* 28cm

 Medium-sized laughingthrush with rufous chestnut upperparts, slightly scaled black and greyish white underparts and white vent. Throat is rufous, bare orbital skin bright blue or reddish and the lores and area around base of bill are black. Ear-coverts are black with white streaks. Three outer pairs of tail feathers are tipped white. The call is a clear loud whistle. It is a common bird living in small groups in the undergrowth of evergreen forests at moderate altitudes in Taiwan.

Spot-breasted Laughingthrush *Garrulax merulinus* 24cm

 Olive-brown laughingthrush with black streaking on breast and faint white line behind eye. Distinguished from Hwamei by grey bill, bolder streaking on breast and lack of white eye-ring. The vent is dark cinnamon. This species' song is even more melodious than that of the famous Hwamei and sounds similar to the European Blackbird's (hence scientific name). Its distribution, however, is much more limited in China, and it is rarely found in the cagebird markets. Ground-feeding groups live in scrub and dense cover of secondary forest and gardens in south-west China and probably south-east Tibet.

Hwamei *Garrulax canorus* 22cm

Unmistakable smallish rufous-brown laughingthrush with diagnostic blue eye-ring and white line behind eye. Chinese name means 'beautiful brow'. Crown and nape finely streaked black. Taiwan race lacks white eye-marks and is more heavily streaked. This species lives in pairs or small parties and is rather shy, keeping to dense cover. It is a familiar cagebird in China because of its beautiful varied and rich song of lively clear whistles. This is a common lowland bird of scrub and gardens over most of south, central and south-east China, including Taiwan and Hainan.

White-browed Laughingthrush *Garrulax sannio* 25cm

Unmistakable greyish-brown laughingthrush with diagnostic buffy-white face pattern and rufous undertail-coverts. Pale eyebrow and cheeks are divided behind eye by brown stripe. Races vary slightly in colour: birds from south-west China have very white face markings, those from central China are more olive in plumage. Has various ringing and buzzing calls and discordant group cackling.

Birds live in pairs or small groups and are not too shy. A common bird of scrub, bamboo thickets and forest edge over much of south-west, central and southern China at moderate elevations.

Scaly Laughingthrush *Garrulax subunicolor* 23cm

Rufous olive-brown laughingthrush scaled over entire body with black feather edges. Central tail feathers are rufous-brown, outer tail feathers are black with white tips. Eyes are yellow, bill is black. Distinguished from Blue-winged Laughingthrush by lack of rufous feather tips, straw rather than blue edges to primaries and lack of black eyebrow. Favours dense scrub and bamboo thickets, but habits otherwise typical of genus. The call is a loud, clear four-note whistle. This is a less common bird in montane forests above 1,800m in the Himalayas to south-west China.

Black-faced Laughingthrush *Garrulax affinis* 26cm

Dark laughingthrush with blackish head with characteristic white malar stripe and white spot behind eye. Faint pale neck bar contrasts against darker background. Body colour varies among races, but is generally dull olive-brown. Wing and tail feathers are edged blue. The call is a monotonous loud three-noted *to–wee–you*. Groups also give whirring alarm calls and emit constant harsh scolding notes as they flit about in the undergrowth of dense montane forests. The bird is a common inhabitant of highest-altitude forests of the Himalayas to central China. There are several races.

Red-winged Laughingthrush *Garrulax formosus* 28cm

Beautiful greyish-brown laughingthrush with crimson-red wings and red edges to tail feathers. Separated from Red-tailed Laughingthrush by grey crown streaked black, blackish sides of head and browner breast. Separated from Red-faced Liocichla by lack of red on side of face. Lives in noisy active groups, usually on or near forest floor and keeping to dense thickets. This is a rare bird, known only from south-west Sichuan and adjacent parts of Yunnan and Guizhou in moist montane forests above 1,800m.

Red-tailed Laughingthrush *Garrulax milnei* 25m

Beautiful laughingthrush with scarlet wings and tail. Ear-coverts are bluish-grey. Distinguished from Red-winged Laughingthrush by rufous-orange crown, lack of black ring around ear-coverts and generally brighter plumage. Mantle and breast are grey with black scalloping pattern. Races vary in plumage details. Birds give loud strident calls as well as group chatters. Jerks tail and flicks wings during noisy dancing display. Groups keep to dense undergrowth in montane evergreen forests of south and south-east China. Rather scarce and shy.

Red-faced Liocichla *Liocichla phoenicea* 23cm

Unmistakable pretty liocichla with scarlet face and primaries and very square-cut, blackish-grey tail with narrow orange tips. Tertials are black with narrow white tips. Easily distinguished from Red-winged and Red-tailed Laughingthrushes by red on face. The call is a loud musical *chi–chweew* or *tu–reew–ri*; also makes low churring notes whilst foraging. A shy bird of dense undergrowth in evergreen montane forests at up to 2,200m, showing some shift in altitude with season. The species is confined to Yunnan province and is rather rare.

Omeishan Liocichla *Liocichla omeiensis* 21cm

Small, pretty, greyish liocichla with colourful wings and tail. Forehead, eyebrow and side of neck are olive-yellow. Tail is olive-grey with fine black bars, cut very square and tipped red. Undertail-coverts are black with orange-red tips, giving barred effect. Wing has bright rufous bar and yellow edges to black primaries. Tertials are black with narrow yellow tips. The bird gives clear loud calls. This is a narrow-range endemic confined to montane forests of Mt Emei and nearby mountains in south-west Sichuan province. It is locally quite common.

111

Silver-eared Mesia *Leiothrix argentauris* 18cm

 Small, colourful babbler with black crown and face contrasting with broad white patch over ear-coverts. Chin, throat, underparts and nape collar yellow on female, orange on male. Primaries are edged bright yellow, with red bases forming a wingbar. Rump is red and tail is edged yellow. Bill and forehead yellow. A noisy flocking bird which gives a variety of loud descending whistles and rattling calls. It often forms mixed-species flocks. It is a common bird of forest edge and secondary forest at up to 2,000m in south-east Tibet and southern China.

Red-billed Leiothrix *Leiothrix lutea* 15cm

 Pretty and colourful little babbler with conspicuous red bill. Upperparts olive-green with yellow patch around eye, underparts orange-yellow. Tail blackish and slightly forked. Wing is blackish, with red and yellow edges forming conspicuous bars at rest. Has a fine but rather monotonous song. Resting birds sit pressed close together and groom each other. Lives in noisy chattering flocks in undergrowth of secondary forests over much of east-central and southern China. A favoured cagebird because of its active singing, beauty and 'loving' habits.

Spectacled Barwing *Actinodura ramsayi* 21cm

Reddish-brown babbler with slight crest and bold white eye-ring. Wings and tail are finely barred black and there is a large rufous patch in wings at base of flight feathers. Underparts dull cinnamon without streaks. Distinguished from other Chinese barwings by white eye-ring and scaled body feathers. Call is a loud but mournful *tu–tui–tui–tui–tuuui*, rising then falling in pitch. Erects crest when calling from tops of small bushes. A fairly common, noisy and lively bird in scrubby forest at altitudes above 900m in southern China.

Streaked Barwing *Actinodura souliei* 23cm

Large floppy crested barwing with scaling on body feathers. Lores and forecheeks black. Crest and ear-coverts are pale grey. Sides of head dark chestnut, mantle and rump grey, throat reddish chestnut. Feathers of back, abdomen and vent are black, lanceolate and edged cinnamon. Wing and tail chestnut with fine black barring. Outer tail feathers broadly tipped white. Voice is soft contact calls or harsh loud churring alarm notes. An uncommon but noisy bird of deciduous forest undergrowth between 1,200–2,500m on mountains of southern China.

Blue-winged Minla *Minla cyanouroptera* 16cm

Unmistakable long-tailed arboreal babbler with blue wings, tail and crown. Mantle, flanks and rump buffish, throat and belly whitish, cheeks greyish. There is a black border above white eyebrow and eye-ring. Tail is white with black edge from below, and rather long, slender and square-cut. Call is a loud, long two-note whistle, *see–saw*, repeated endlessly, rising in pitch at end of call. Lives in small active flocks working through upper and lower canopies of upland forests in southern China.

Chestnut-tailed Minla *Minla strigula* 16cm

Active tit-like babbler with erectile rufous crown, black and white or yellow scaly pattern on throat, yellowish underparts and olive upperparts. Primaries are edged yellow to give colourful panel and tail is centrally rufous, subterminally and laterally black, tipped and edged yellow. Lives in flocks and joins 'bird waves'. Voice is a slurred whistle, *chu–u– wee*, *chu–u–wee*, with second note falling, otherwise on rising pitch. This is a common inquisitive bird, keeping to lower trees and bushes of montane broadleaf and conifer forests of Himalayas, south Tibet and central and south-west China.

114

Red-tailed Minla *Minla ignotincta* 14cm

Male has broad white eyebrow contrasting with black crown, nape and broad eye-stripe and with red edges to tail and primaries. Back is grey, wings otherwise black with white edges, tail centrally black and underparts white with creamy tinge. Female and juvenile have yellow wing panel and edge of tail pink. Has loud plaintive call of three or four notes. This is a common flock-living bird, working through lower crowns and undergrowth in oak forests of Himalayas, south Tibet and central and southern China.

Grey-cheeked Fulvetta *Alcippe morrisonia* 14cm

Noisy inquisitive flock-living fulvetta. Upperparts brown, head grey and underparts greyish-buff. Has conspicuous white eye-ring. Black eye-stripe varies from prominent to barely visible. Distinguished from Brown-cheeked Fulvetta by whiter underparts, greyer cheeks and white eye-ring. Call is an agitated churring when disturbed. Readily attracted by 'pishing'. These birds are aggressive in mobbing small owls and other raptors. This is a common bird in south and central China, Hainan and Taiwan, often mixed with other species in 'bird waves'.

115

Black-headed Sibia *Heterophasia melanoleuca* 22cm

Long-tailed grey sibia with black head, tail and wings. Crested crown is glossy. Tail is tipped grey on central feathers and white on outer feathers. Throat and central underparts are white, but flanks are smoky-grey. Race in extreme south-west Yunnan has brownish back. Call is five-note song with three notes on same pitch and last two lower. Habits are similar to those of a malcoha or squirrel, creeping about among mossy epiphytes in a rather skulking and jerky manner. This is a common bird in montane forests of south-central and south China above 1,200m.

White-eared Sibia *Heterophasia auricularis* 23cm

Unmistakable arboreal babbler with black crown and unique white eye-stripe, protracted backwards and upwards and ending in long-spreading filamentous plumes. Throat, breast and upper back grey; rest of underparts pinkish-cinnamon, lower back and rump rufous. Tail black, with central feathers tipped whitish. Call is resonant repeated *fei fei fei…*, rising at the end, or rattling *de de de de*. Sometimes gathers in small parties to feed in fruiting and flowering trees. Active and not so shy. A common endemic bird of the oak forests of Taiwan at moderate altitudes.

Long-tailed Sibia *Heterophasia picaoides* 30cm

Grey sibia with extremely long graduated and pointed tail with barred white feather tips. Upperparts dark grey, underparts pale grey. Bill is black, feet are grey and iris is red. Black wings have prominent white patch. Distinguished from Black-capped Sibia by lack of black crown. It has a loud, clear ringing call. Lives in small flocks that glide from tree to tree. This is a fairly common bird in montane oak forests above 1,500m in south-west China in Yunnan province.

Striated Yuhina *Yuhina castaniceps* 13cm

Active yuhina with grey upperparts, white underparts and characteristic chestnut cheeks extending as nuchal collar. Has slight forward-bending crest and upperparts finely streaked with white feather shafts. Tail is dark brownish-grey with white edge. Voice is continuous *ser–weet ser–weet*. This is a common bird generally found in small noisy flocks actively searching for insects through the lower forest canopy. Often forms mixed flocks with other species. Distributed along Himalayas and through south and east China at 600–1,500m.

117

Stripe-throated Yuhina *Yuhina gularis* 15cm

Dull brown yuhina with prominent crest, black streaking on pinkish-buff throat and orange-rufous streak in black wing. Rest of underparts are dull rufous-buff. There is a concealed white patch at side of neck. Omeishan race is paler, with rufous-brown crest. The call is a distinct nasal mewing. Flocks mix with other species in 'bird waves' and work busily through the crowns of flowering trees. A common flock-living bird in montane broadleaf forests above 1,200m in the Himalayas, south-east Tibet, and south-central and south-west China.

Rufous-vented Yuhina *Yuhina occipitalis* 13cm

Small brown yuhina with prominent grey and orange crest. Has greyish upper mantle and black moustachial streak. Underparts are pinkish-buff with rufous undertail-coverts. Has white eye-ring. Bill is pinkish and legs are orange. Gives a short buzzing call note. This is a common flock-living bird, often mixing with other species. Occurs in montane mossy forest from 2,300m to 3,600m in the Himalayas and mountains of south-east Tibet and south-west China. Comes to lower altitudes in winter.

Black-chinned Yuhina *Yuhina nigrimenta* 12cm

 Small greyish yuhina with short crest, grey head, olive-grey upperparts and whitish underparts. Has black forehead and lores and diagnostic black chin. Lower bill is red and feet are yellow-orange. This is a common, gregarious bird of montane forest canopy. Emits constant squeaky chatter. Sometimes mixes with other species in large flocks. Distributed from south-east Tibet to central and southern China. Lives around forest clearings, forest and secondary scrub at up to 2000m in summer, but comes down as low as 300m in winter.

Black-throated Tit *Aegithalos concinnus* 10cm

 Small, active, elegant tit. Different races vary. Crown and nape rufous or greyish, broad eye-stripe black, chin and throat white with round black bib. Underparts white with varying amounts of chestnut on breast bar and flanks. Mantle and wings grey and tail blackish with white edges. Juvenile has buff crown. Call is very shrill *tweet tweet* and low churring notes. A common bird of broadleaf and conifer forests at up to 3,300m in the Himalayas, south-east Tibet, central and south-east China and Taiwan.

119

Long-tailed Tit *Aegithalos caudatus* 16cm

Beautiful fluffy little tit with tiny black bill and very long white-edged black tail. Different races vary in colour pattern. Birds in north-east China are almost completely white-bodied, whilst those in Yangtze valley have a broad black brow, brown and black wing pattern and pinkish tinge on the underparts. Long-tailed Tits live in small active flocks, feeding on insects and some seeds. The call is a thin metallic trill *seehwi-wiwiwi*. Birds also give dry churring calls and a high-pitched *seeh–seeh–seeh* as they work through the canopy. Common in open forest and forest edges over north, east and central China.

Coal Tit *Parus ater* 10cm

Small tit with black crown, sides of neck, throat and upper breast. There is a large white patch on the nape. Back is grey or olive-grey and belly is white with or without buff. Some races have a pointed black crest. Wings are black with two conspicuous wingbars and paler edges to primaries. Tail is blackish with feathers edged grey. White nuchal patch distinguishes the species from Willow and Marsh Tits, and distinguished from Great and Green-backed Tits by lack of black breast stripe. Common in conifer forests from Tibet to north and central China and mountains of south-east China.

120

Great Tit *Parus major* 14cm

Large plump tit with glossy black head contrasting with white cheeks and white nape patch. Has black band down centre of underparts, broader on male. Tail is mostly black, with central feathers grey and outer feathers edged white. Some races have greenish-olive back and yellowish underparts. South-eastern races are grey on the back and have whitish underparts. Distinguished from Green-backed Tit by lack of blue in wings and tail. Calls very variable and loud, including characteristic three-note *tee tee tu* with the stressed last note dipping and rising again. Common over the whole country.

Eurasian Nuthatch *Sitta europaea* 13cm

Smart-coloured nuthatch with bluish-grey upperparts, black eye-stripe, white throat, buffish belly and rich chestnut flanks. Gives loud sharp *seet, seet* calls, scolding *twet–twet,twet* and musical whistled song. Creeps about on tree trunks and branches working generally downwards searching for insects. Clings to bark with one foot held above body. Acorns and nuts are drilled in crevices and holes in tree trunks. Flight is jerky and undulating. Occasionally feeds on ground. Lives in pairs or small flocks. Rather common in deciduous woodlands over much of the country.

Common Treecreeper *Certhiola familiaris* 14cm

Mottled brown bird with long, slightly decurved bill usually creeping about on the trunks and branches of trees. Underparts buff with rufous flanks and tail coverts. Whitish breast and flanks distinguish it from the Rusty-flanked Treecreeper, smaller size and pale throat distinguish it from Brown-throated Treecreeper. Plain brown tail distinguishes from Bar-tailed Treecreeper. Call is loud *cheet cheet*. Feeding birds work quietly upwards to the top of the tree then fly to the base of another tree and start again. Common in coniferous and mixed forests across most of northern China as far south as northern Yunnan.

Fire-tailed Sunbird *Aethopyga ignicauda* 20cm

Adult (above); immature (right)

Male an unmistakable red sunbird with greatly elongated bright scarlet central tail feathers. Crown is metallic blue; lores, side of head black; throat and moustachial streak metallic purple. Underparts yellow, with bright orange patch on breast. The female is greyish-olive with a yellow rump, and much smaller than the male. The call is a quiet shrill note, *shweet*. This most beautiful of sunbirds is confined to the mountains of south-west China and southern Tibet, where it feeds on the flowers of rhododendrons, brambles and flowering bushes at moderate altitudes in conifer forests. It is not so rare in suitable habitat.

Fork-tailed Sunbird *Aethopyga christinae* 10cm

Small dainty sunbird. Crown and nape metallic green, upperparts olive or blackish with yellow rump. Uppertail-coverts and central tail feathers glossy metallic green; central two tail feathers have slender elongated points. Outer tail feathers are black, tipped white. Side of head is black with iridescent green moustachial stripe and maroon throat patch. Underparts otherwise dirty olive-white. Female is very small, with olive upperparts and pale greenish-yellow underparts. This is a common bird in south-east and south China and Hainan, living in forest and wooded areas, even in towns, visiting flowering bushes and trees.

Streaked Spiderhunter *Arachnothera magna* 19cm

Large, heavily streaked spiderhunter with bright orange legs. Feathers of upperparts are olive with black centres, giving bold streaking. Underparts yellowish-white, streaked with black. The eye is brown and the very long decurved bill is black. Birds are fiercely territorial and engage in noisy chases, giving a characteristic sharp *cheet* call in fast flight. This is a common bird in the lower canopy of dense evergreen lowland and hill forests, especially where wild bananas or gingers abound. It feeds mostly on the flowers of these plants, piercing through the base of the flowers to drain out nectar.

123

Japanese White-eye *Zosterops japonicus* 10cm

Attractive small flocking bird with bright green-olive upperparts, conspicuous white eye-ring and yellow throat and vent. Breast and flanks are grey, with white abdomen. Lacks chestnut flanks of Chestnut-flanked White-eye and ventral yellow band of Oriental White-eye. Active and noisy bird of tree crowns, feeding on small insects, tiny fruits and nectar. Birds constantly emit soft *tzee* note and quiet trills. Breeds in east and central China, migrating south in winter, where it is rather common in woodlands, forest edge, parks and towns. Often captured as a cagebird.

Black-naped Oriole *Oriolus chinensis* 26cm

Bright yellow oriole with black eye-line and black in wing and tail. Bill is pink. Female is similar to male, but duller and slightly streaked. Juvenile has heavily streaked white underparts. Distinguished from Slender-billed Oriole by thicker bill and broader black band around nape. The call is a clear, fluty *we–weeleow* and harsh nasal mewing. Favours woodland, secondary forest and gardens, restlessly searching for insects and fruits in the tree canopy. Flight is slightly undulating. This is a common bird which breeds in north and central China and winters in the south.

Black-hooded Oriole *Oriolus xanthornus* 21cm

Unmistakable yellow oriole with entire head, throat and upper breast black. Rest of plumage is bright yellow except for black of wings and tail. Bill is pink and eye red. Female is like male, but tinged olive above. Immature is similar to adult, but with yellowish forehead, whitish eye-ring and black streaks on whitish throat. The call is similar to that of Black-naped Oriole, a three- or four-noted *tu–hu–a–yu*. This is a common bird of lowland forests in Indochina, but in China is confined to south-east Tibet and south Yunnan. Keeps to the canopy of large trees. Frequents open woodlands and orchards.

Long-tailed Shrike *Lanius schach* 25cm

A shrike with a very long tail, distinguished by a black mask, grey crown and nape with rufous back and black wings, usually with a notable white wing patch. Separated from the Grey-backed Shrike by rufous back, longer tail, and white wing patch if present. Shrikes sit on prominent poles, fences or terminal treetops to scold with harsh strident calls. They feed on large insects and even small vertebrates. They are also fiercely territorial and engage in shrieking chases. A common and noisily self-advertising bird of open scrub, forest edge and gardens over much of eastern and southern China.

125

Grey-backed Shrike *Lanius tephronotus* 23cm

Similar to the Long-tailed Shrike, but distinguished by dark grey back with only a narrow rufous-buff band across the rump and upper-tail-coverts. General behaviour, diet and screeching, strident calls are similar to those of the Long-tailed Shrike, which it replaces in Tibet and central China, with some overlap in the latter. This species lives at up to 4,500m in the Himalayas, where it is locally rather common in scrub, open areas and cultivated lands. It is quite tame.

Spangled Drongo *Dicrurus hottentotus* 32cm

Glossy black drongo with greenish sheen. Has diagnostic upturned blunt, lyre-shaped outer tail feathers and crest of long filaments on forehead. Voice consists of harsh grating and scolding and loud metallic 'creaking-gate' calls. This is an active bird, hawking insects from prominent perch and making swooping fluttery flights through the canopy. Aggressively mobs and chases crows and birds of prey. At dusk, flies up into sky to join other drongos in aerial display flights and chases. Males fly vertically upwards before spiralling down on arched wings. This is a common bird of lowland forests in central and south China.

Greater Racket-tailed Drongo *Dicrurus paradiseus* 46cm

Large glossy black drongo with prominent crest, very forked tail and elongated, long-shafted rackets on outer tail feathers. Distinguished from Lesser Racket-tailed Drongo by longer crest, curled rackets and more deeply forked tail. Calls include a wide range of loud clear whistles and a musical song with harsh grating notes. Sits on prominent perch, often in shady place in lower canopy, to hawk after insects in swooping flight. Aggressively mobs crows and birds of prey. A common forest bird in south-east Tibet, south-west and south China and Hainan.

Eurasian Jay *Garrulus glandarius* 35cm

Small pinkish crow with diagnostic black and electric-blue patterned wing panel and white rump. Moustachial stripe is black and wings are black with white patch. This is a noisy bird of deciduous woodlands and forest. The call is a harsh shout, *ksher*, or plaintive mewing. Wings in flight are broad and rounded. Flies with laboured irregular beats. Jays feed on fruits, birds' eggs and carrion, and are major consumers of acorns. They are bold mobsters of raptors. Widespread and quite common over much of northern, central and eastern China.

127

Blue Magpie *Urocissa erythrorhyncha* 68cm

Long-tailed bright blue magpie with a white-crowned black head. Distinguished from Golden-billed Magpie by scarlet bill and red feet. Abdomen and vent are white, and the outer tail feathers are graduated and black with white tips. This is a noisy bird which lives in small flocks. It feeds on fruits, insects and carrion and often feeds on the ground. Birds give harsh screeched contact calls plus a wide range of other calls and whistles. Aggressively mob raptors. This is a common and widespread species of forest edge, scrub and even villages.

Azure-winged Magpie *Cyanopica cyana* 35cm

Small, slender, grey crow with black hood, azure-bluish wings and long blue tail. Lives in noisy groups in open pine and broadleaf woodlands, parkland and even towns. Call is a harsh rolling *zhruee* or clear *kwee*. Flight is characterized by quick wingbeats interspersed by long silent glides. Birds feed on fruits, insects and carrion in trees, on ground and off tree trunks. Flocks frequently raid persimmon plantations in autumn. Common and widespread in east and north-east China. Introduced into Hong Kong but declining there.

Rufous Treepie *Dendrocitta vagabunda* 44cm

Rufous-brown crow with long graduated grey tail and pale whitish wing patch, readily distinguishing it from Grey Treeepie and Collared Treepie. Face is black, grading into grey crown, nape and breast. Back and rump are rufous-brown and underparts are rufous-buff. Bill is grey and eyes red. Keeps to crowns of small trees and hunts insects and small vertebrates. Call is raucous ringing *bob–a–link*. The most southerly of China's three treepies. Common in scrub and forest at up to 2,000m in south-west China and probably south-east Tibet.

Ratchet-tailed Treepie *Temnurus temnurus* 30cm

Unmistakable small black crow with unique 'pagoda'-patterned ratchet tail. Head is black and body dark grey. The head is thick and the bill heavy and decurved. The species makes an amazing range of extraordinary cranking and honking calls and whistles. It lives in small flocks that work steadily through the canopy, feeding on insects and fruits. Flight is flappy and clumsy, but also makes long glides like a malcoha. Common in the forest of Indochina but occurs in China only on Hainan island, where it now appears to be rather rare.

129

Unmistakable pied crow with long black tail. Black of wings and tail have bluish gloss. Bill and feet black. It is a highly adaptable bird, as much at home in the open farmland of northern China as in the high-rise skyscrapers of Hong Kong. Call is a rolling harsh cackle. It is an omnivorous scrounger, but feeds mostly on the ground. It lives in small parties. The nest is a domed and irregular pile of sticks; the same nest is used year after year. A widespread and common bird in China, where it is regarded as bringing good luck and is generally not persecuted.

Red-billed Chough *Pyrrhocorax pyrrhocorax* 43cm

Smart, smallish black crow with short, bright red decurved bill and red feet. Young birds as adult, but bill is blacker. Distinguished from Alpine Chough by shorter, red rather than yellow bill. Very agile in flight, playing on thermals and gliding with short broad wings and prominent 'fingers' of spread primaries. Call is a harsh sharp *kee–ach*. It lives in small to large groups and is often found around buildings and farms at moderate to high altitudes over much of the Tibetan plateau and Himalayas, or at lower altitudes in the north-east.

House Crow *Corvus splendens* 42cm

Medium-sized black crow with sleek outline. Distinguished from other black crows by grey neck, breast and upper back. Distinguished from jackdaws by larger size and more powerful bill. The call is a high-pitched rasping *ka* or lower-pitched *kowk*. The House Crow is a commensal of man and lives in large flocks around villages and rubbish tips. The species also lives in woodlands and often roosts in noisy flocks in large trees. This is a common bird in south-central China and Tibet up to quite high altitudes.

Carrion Crow *Corvus corone* 46cm

Large black crow, distinguished from Rook by black feathered base to bill and from Thick-billed Crow by low-browed profile and more slender though still powerful bill. The call is a harsh croaking *kraa*. Gathers in large roosting flocks, but does not nest in colonies like Rooks. This bird feeds in short grassland and agricultural fields. It eats mostly invertebrates but is fond of carrion, and is frequently seen on roads feeding on road kills. Does not generally move into urban habitats as does Thick-billed Crow.

Large-billed Crow *Corvus macrorhynchos* 54cm

Large glossy black crow, distinguished from Carrion Crow by higher brow and thicker, less pointed bill. Upper mandible of bill strongly curved. Distinguished from Raven by smaller size, rounder tail and less deep call. The call is a harsh throaty *kwaa*. It forms small flocks and is a notorious scavenger. Often feeds on road kills, and sometimes mixes with Collared Crow in bare river beds or cultivated areas. This is a common crow of woodlands, forests, mangroves and even towns and villages over most of Tibet, north-east, central and south China, Hainan and Taiwan at up to 3,000m.

White-shouldered Starling *Sturnus sinensis* 20cm

Silky pale grey starling with whitish crown and dark wings and tail. Male has entire shoulder of wing white, and often has rusty tinge on white parts of plumage. Female has only broad white bar on shoulder. Grey bill and pale tip to tail distinguish this species from Silky Starling. Call is shrill chatter when feeding. Lives in small to large flocks which feed in fruiting trees and rarely on the ground. This is a widespread species in southern China, Hainan and Taiwan in farmland and gardens. Shows some seasonal migrations.

132

Common Starling *Sturnus vulgaris* 20cm

Blackish starling glossed purplish-green, with various degrees of white spotting. Fresh feathers of body are lanceolate in shape with rusty edges, giving a scalloped and spotted pattern which mostly disappears with wear. The calls are harsh screeches and whistles. Lives in small to large flocks and feeds on the ground in open areas. This is a common bird in western China in cultivated areas, around towns and on edges of desert. Congregates in winter into large flocks, which migrate to southern limits of range. Occasional migrants are found in east China.

Asian Pied Starling *Sturnus contra* 24cm

Smaller pied starling with black head and neck and white cheeks. Belly, rump and wingbar are white, but plumage otherwise black. Distinguished from larger Black-collared Starling by black nape and throat, orange-based white bill, orange orbital skin and lack of white tip to tail. Call is harsh screeches and whistles. This is a common bird of open grassland and farmland, feeding on the ground in small flocks, often near cattle. In China this species is confined to the south-west, in Yunnan province and probably south-east Tibet.

Black-collared Starling *Sturnus nigricollis* 28cm

Large black and white starling. Head white, with black collar and breast. Back and wings black with white edging. Tail black with white tip. Bare skin around eye and legs yellow. Female like male but browner. Juvenile lacks black collar. Distinguished from Asian Pied Starling by larger size, white throat and crown, yellow orbital skin, lack of clear white wingbar and black bill. Call is harsh screeches and whistles. A common bird of farmland in southern China, generally feeding on the ground in small flocks in paddy fields, grazing areas or open ground. Sometimes feeds among herds of buffalo or cattle.

Common Myna *Acridotheres tristis* 25cm

Jaunty brownish myna with dark head and breast, white wing flash, and diagnostic white wing lining visible in flight. Bare skin around eye and feet are yellow. Vent and tip of tail are white. Has no crest. Voice is harsh screeches, whistles and liquid gurgling notes. Lives in flocks and feeds on ground in rice fields, parks and grassy areas. This is a common bird in open farmland areas and cities in south-east Tibet and south and south-west China at up to 3,000m. Feral populations have become established in some southern cities, including Hong Kong.

Crested Myna *Acridotheres cristatellus* 26cm

Large black myna with long frontal crest. Similar to White-vented Myna, but distinguished by larger size, ivory-coloured bill with rosy base, and black undertail-coverts (only narrowly scaled with white). White wing flash conspicuous in flight. Has narrow white tip to tail. Immature is browner. Often feeds around and perches on cattle. Voice is loud and variable; it is a good mimic of other birds and can be taught to talk. This is a common bird of lowland agricultural areas, feeding on ground in open paddy fields and grassy or open areas and gardens.

Hill Myna *Gracula religiosa* 30cm

Large glossy, arboreal myna with orange bill, yellow feet and diagnostic golden fleshy lappets on the side of head. White wing patch conspicuous in flight against otherwise all-black plumage. Call a very loud, piercing *tiong* and whistles; often mimics other birds calls. This is a popular cagebird that can be trained to talk. Generally lives in pairs, but sometimes forms small flocks. Regular visitor to fruiting fig trees. This is a common bird of evergreen forest in south-east Tibet and south-west China and Hainan. Feral population occurs in Hong Kong.

135

Russet Sparrow *Passer rutilans* 14cm

Brightly coloured sparrow. Male has bright cinnamon or chestnut crown and upperparts, black streaking on mantle, black throat and dirty white cheeks. Female is duller, with broad dark eyestripe and long creamy supercilium. Calls include a single *cheep*, rapid *chit–chit–chit* or repeated song, *cheep–chirrup–cheweep*. This is a common flock-living bird in rural areas at higher altitudes over most of China in open forests, forest edge and cultivated areas. Flocks feed on grass seeds, grain, small fruits and insects. In absence of House Sparrow, this species also lives around villages.

Eurasian Tree-Sparrow *Passer montanus* 14cm

Plump, lively sparrow with brownish upperparts and buff underparts. Has complete whitish collar around nape. Distinguished from House Sparrow and Russet Sparrow by chocolate-maroon crown and conspicuous black ear spot. Black of throat less extensive. Female resembles male. The call is a chirpy hard *cheep cheep*, also given in flight. Regularly mixes with other species of seed-eating birds. This is a common bird in lightly wooded areas, villages and farmland over much of China and can become a pest of grain crops. Replaces the House Sparrow as the 'city' sparrow in the east of the country.

Grey-capped Greenfinch *Carduelis sinica* 13cm

Attractive olive-brown finch. Male has grey cap and nape, uniform brown back and bright yellow patches in wing and at base of tail. Female is duller, and juvenile is paler and more streaked. Distinguished from the Black-headed Greenfinch by lack of dark head pattern and darker underparts. Flight call is twittering *dzidzi–i–dzi–i*. Song is like that of Greenfinch. Wintering flocks sometimes number hundreds of birds. Feeds in trees and on ground on many kinds of seeds, fruits and insects. This is a common bird of wooded valleys, scrub and farmland over much of eastern China, especially in conifer forests and along river banks.

Plain Mountain-finch *Leucosticte nemoricola* 15cm

Sparrow-like finch, brown with pale streaking, light supercilium and thin white or creamy wingbars. There is no white in tail. Sexes alike, but juvenile is a warmer brown than adult. Distinguished from Brandt's Mountain-finch by paler head and lack of pink tips to feathers of rump. Voice is soft *chi–chi–chi–chi*, or song of *dui–dip–dip–dip* given from prominent rock. Lives in large flocks on alpine meadows at high altitudes, actively running about on the ground. Flies in wheeling flocks with fast changes of direction. Common and found throughout Himalayas and highlands of west and central China.

White-browed Rosefinch *Carpodacus thura* 17cm

Male (above); female (below)

Large, brightly coloured rosefinch. Male has deep pink rump and crown, with long pale pink eyebrow becoming white posteriorly. White tips to median wing-coverts give slight wingbar. Female is distinguished from other female rosefinches by deep yellow rump and warm brown on breast. Feeds in flocks in grassy and open areas in forest through the winter, and in scrub along the treeline through the summer months. The calls include loud sharp whistles, rapid piping and sharp buzzing *deep–deep, deep–de–de–de*. This is a common and approachable species along the Himalayas and north to Qinghai.

White-winged Grosbeak *Mycerobas carnipes* 23cm

Large, chunky finch with massive grey bill. Male has entire anterior half of body plus tail dull black. Lower back, abdomen and vent are dull dirty yellow. Wing is black with white patch and with yellow edges to tertials and greater coverts. Black is more extensive and yellow less bright than on other grosbeaks. Female is duller and greyer. Call is loud nasal *schwenk* or longer *un di di di dit* song. This is a common bird, living singly or in small parties among the treetops of conifer forests at up to 4,000m along the Himalayas and forested ranges of north-west China.

Crested Bunting *Melophus lathami* 16cm

Male (left); female (right)

Dark bunting with characteristic long thin crest. Male is glossy black with chestnut wings and tail; tip of tail is black. Female is dark olive-brown, heavily streaked on mantle and breast; has smaller crest than male and chestnut edges to dark wing feathers. Lives and feeds mostly on ground, where it is an active and conspicuous bird. Breeds in mountains in summer but winters in valleys, where it often feeds in fields. The call is a quite loud *pit–pit*; also has sweet song. Locally rather common. This is a bird of open ground and short grassland in hilly country over much of China.

Yellow-breasted Bunting *Emberiza aureola* 14cm

Breeding male has black face, chestnut crown and mantle, bright yellow underparts with chestnut breast band and some black streaks on flanks. Back and wings are brown, mottled with black and with a pronounced white bar on the shoulder and finer white bar on wing. Rump is chestnut. Female is similar but duller with yellow eyebrow, chin and side of neck and a dark brown patch on side of face outlined in black. Immature and wintering male resemble female but male has some chestnut on crown. Winter male distinguished from wintering Black-headed Bunting by more prominent white wing patch. Breeds in north-east China wintering to southern provinces in large numbers.

139

Further reading

R.M. de Schauensee *The Birds of China*. Oxford University Press, Oxford, England, 1984

R.D. Etchécopar and F. Hüe *Les Oiseaux de Chine, de Mongolie et de Corée* (Two volumes: *Non-passeraux*, *Passeraux*). Papeete, Tahiti. Editions du Pacifique, 1978 & 1982

Cheng Tso-Hsin *A Distributional List of Chinese Birds*. Rev. ed. Beijing Institute of Zoology, Academia Sinica, 1976

C. Viney, K. Phillipps and C.Y. Lam *Birds of Hong Kong and South China*. Govt of Hongkong Printing Office, Hongkong, 1994

B. King, M. Woodcock and E.C. Dickinson *A Field Guide to the Birds of South-East Asia*. Collins, London, 1975

Index